Houghton
Mifflin
Harcourt

Math

Grade 6

Core Skills Math

GRADE 6

Table of Contents

Table of Contents
Core Skills Math, Grade 6

Table of Contents
Core Skills Math, Grade 6

Common Core State Standards for Mathematics Correlation Chart

Ratios and Proportional Relationships

Understand ratio concepts and use ratio reasoning to solve problems.

6.RP.1	75, 76
6.RP.2	77, 80, 81
6.RP.3	
6.RP.3.a *Supporting Skills*	82, 83, 86 78, 79
6.RP.3.b	84, 85
6.RP.3.c *Supporting Skills*	87, 88, 89, 90, 91, 92, 93, 94, 95, 96, 97 61
6.RP.3.d	67, 68, 69, 70

The Number System

Apply and extend previous understandings of multiplication and division to divide fractions by fractions.

6.NS.1	58, 62, 63, 64, 65, 66

Compute fluently with multi-digit numbers and find common factors and multiples.

6.NS.2	2, 3, 4, 5, 6, 7, 8
6.NS.3	9, 10, 11, 12, 13, 14, 15, 16, 17, 18
6.NS.4 *Supporting Skills*	42, 43, 44, 59 37, 38, 39, 40, 41

Apply and extend previous understandings of numbers to the system of rational numbers.

6.NS.5	109, 110
6.NS.6	
6.NS.6.a	45, 114
6.NS.6.b	51
6.NS.6.c	46, 50, 52
6.NS.7	
6.NS.7.a	47, 112
6.NS.7.b	47, 111
6.NS.7.c	113
6.NS.7.d	115
6.NS.8	49, 53, 60

Expressions and Equations

Apply and extend previous understandings of arithmetic to algebraic expressions.

6.EE.1 *Supporting Skills*	36, 48 35

6.EE.2	
6.EE.2.a	116, 117, 118
6.EE.2.b	119, 120, 121, 122
6.EE.2.c	123, 124, 125, 126
6.EE.3	128, 129, 130, 131, 132
Supporting Skills	1
6.EE.4	133

Reason about and solve one-variable equations and inequalities.

6.EE.5	142, 149
6.EE.6	56, 57
Supporting Skills	55
6.EE.7	134, 135, 136, 137, 138, 139, 140, 141
6.EE.8	147, 148

Represent and analyze quantitative relationships between dependent and independent variables.

6.EE.9	127, 143, 144, 145, 146

Geometry

Solve real-world and mathematical problems involving area, surface area, and volume.

6.G.1	98, 99, 100, 101, 102
6.G.2	103, 107, 108
6.G.3	54, 104
6.G.4	106
Supporting Skills	71, 72, 73, 74, 105

Statistics and Probability

Develop understanding of statistical variability.

6.SP.1	19
6.SP.2	20, 25
6.SP.3	22, 26

Summarize and describe distributions.

6.SP.4	21, 27, 28
6.SP.5	
6.SP.5.a	29
6.SP.5.b	29
6.SP.5.c	23, 24, 30, 31, 32
6.SP.5.d	33, 34

Name _____ Date _____

Dividing with 2-Digit Divisors

Estimate each quotient.

1. $53\overline{)254}$

2. $21\overline{)125}$

3. $71\overline{)5,409}$

4. $12\overline{)1,078}$

_____ _____ _____ _____

5. $78\overline{)394}$

6. $32,688 \div 62$

7. $1,642 \div 24$

8. $36,574 \div 41$

_____ _____ _____ _____

Find each quotient.

9. $83\overline{)598}$

10. $34\overline{)145}$

11. $81\overline{)649}$

12. $91\overline{)743}$

_____ _____ _____ _____

13. $73\overline{)3,572}$

14. $98\overline{)1,959}$

15. $33\overline{)12,841}$

16. $2,066 \div 33$

_____ _____ _____ _____

17. $3,468 \div 72$

18. $25\overline{)1,826}$

19. $38,190 \div 29$

20. $19\overline{)2,540}$

_____ _____ _____ _____

Complete each table.

	Divisor	Dividend	Quotient
21.	24	2,304	
22.	98		97
23.		1,020	85
24.	48		34

	Divisor	Dividend	Quotient
25.	51	1,173	
26.		882	14
27.	34		38
28.	45	405	

MIXED APPLICATIONS

29. Bill has 180 marbles. He puts 27 marbles in each bag. How many bags does he fill?

_____

30. There are 50 pennies in a roll. Janet has 41 rolls of pennies. How many pennies does she have?

_____

5

Dividing Larger Numbers

Estimate each quotient. If the estimate is greater than 1,000, find the quotient.

1. $7\overline{)3,382}$ 2. $4\overline{)2,321}$ 3. $4\overline{)18,948}$ 4. $5\overline{)4,721}$

_____   _____   _____   _____

5. $3\overline{)6,942}$ 6. $6\overline{)5,920}$ 7. $7\overline{)33,956}$ 8. $3\overline{)52,654}$

_____   _____   _____   _____

Estimate. Then find each quotient.

9. $5,321 \div 9 = n$ 10. $38,932 \div 8 = n$ 11. $49,327 \div 7 = n$

_____   _____   _____

MIXED APPLICATIONS

12. The company Ted's father works for bought 4 cars for $36,400. Each car cost the same amount. How much did each car cost?

_____

13. Alfredo collects coins. He has filled 4 albums that each hold 1,632 coins. He has 511 loose coins. How many coins does he have?

_____

MIXED REVIEW

Find each missing factor. Name the property used.

14. $(6 \times 4) \times$ _____ $= 6 \times (4 \times 5)$

_____

15. $(3 \times 5) + (3 \times 7) =$ _____ $\times (5 + 7)$

_____

Zeros in the Quotient

Find each quotient.

1. $21\overline{)4{,}221}$

2. $17\overline{)527}$

3. $19\overline{)1{,}729}$

4. $23\overline{)23{,}920}$

5. $31\overline{)18{,}600}$

6. $27\overline{)18{,}927}$

7. $32\overline{)2{,}368}$

8. $33\overline{)34{,}044}$

9. $42\overline{)55{,}041}$

10. $47\overline{)4{,}324}$

11. $49\overline{)58{,}849}$

12. $50\overline{)35{,}010}$

MIXED APPLICATIONS

13. The members of a knitting club made 700 dolls. They sold the dolls for $3 each and gave the money to a senior citizens' center. In the first week, they sold $1,860 worth of dolls. How many dolls did they have left?

14. A theater is selling tickets for $40 for 1 person or $150 for 4 people. How much can a class of 200 students save by buying tickets at the group price?

NUMBER SENSE

Compare. Write $<$ or $>$ in each circle.

15. $5{,}484 \div 12$ ◯ $5{,}484 \div 17$

16. $8{,}232 \div 14$ ◯ $6{,}232 \div 14$

17. $2{,}078 \div 26$ ◯ $5{,}092 \div 26$

18. $5{,}856 \div 31$ ◯ $5{,}856 \div 11$

Division: Using Inverse Operations

Use inverse operations to complete each table.

	Divisor	Dividend	Quotient
1.	35	21,140	
2.		5,025	1,005
3.	6		80 r2

	Divisor	Dividend	Quotient
4.	63	12,852	
5.	27		208
6.	6		50 r4

Find each quotient.

7. $9\overline{)3,606}$ **8.** $8\overline{)2,560}$ **9.** $6\overline{)9,600}$ **10.** $3\overline{)6,211}$

_____   _____   _____   _____

11. $14\overline{)4,231}$ **12.** $24\overline{)4,900}$ **13.** $67\overline{)23,452}$ **14.** $33\overline{)2,977}$

_____   _____   _____   _____

MIXED APPLICATIONS

15. Manuel has 120 pages in his stamp album. Each page holds 6 stamps. How many stamps does he have?

_____

16. Masalina's store sold 480 erasers. In all, 80 boxes of erasers were sold. If the number of erasers in each box was the same, how many erasers were in each box?

_____

MIXED REVIEW

Determine whether each number is divisible by 2, 3, 5, 9, and 10. Write all that apply.

17. 560 _____   **18.** 245 _____   **19.** 6,072 _____   **20.** 4,545 _____

Choose the best estimate. Circle *a*, *b*, or *c*.

21. $9\overline{)452}$

 a. 70   **b.** 50   **c.** 35

22. $27\overline{)25,230}$

 a. 2,000   **b.** 1,000   **c.** 3,000

Find each quotient.

23. $8\overline{)736}$ **24.** $1,560 \div 5$ **25.** $63\overline{)1,071}$ **26.** $703 \div 57$

_____   _____   _____   _____

Adding Decimals

Place the decimal point in each sum.

1. $6.3 + 0.26 + 14.816 = 2\ 1\ 3\ 7\ 6$

2. $7.069 + 4.274 + 13.5 = 2\ 4\ 8\ 4\ 3$

3. $32.09 + 8.027 + 16.8 = 5\ 6\ 9\ 1\ 7$

4. $0.2 + 324.529 + 26.93 = 3\ 5\ 1\ 6\ 5\ 9$

Find each sum.

5. $4.3 + 1.5 = \underline{5.8}$

6. $23.82 + 18.8 = \underline{4262}$

7. $9.606 + 0.42 = \underline{10.026}$

8. $\$54.20 + \$5.93 = \underline{\$60.13}$

9. $65.03 + 7.468 = \underline{72.498}$

10. $13.076 + 0.08 = \underline{13.156}$

11.
```
  2.781
 13.284
+ 6.63
-------
 22.695
```
(22.695)

12.
```
 43.17
  2.899
+ 17.4
-------
 63.469
```
(63.469)

13.
```
  7.521
 40.28
+ 0.1684
-------
 47.9694
```
(47.9694)

14.
```
  4.7
 21.58
+ 4.123
-------
 30.403
```
(30.403)

15.
```
  14.9
 621.8
+ 26.93
-------
 663.63
```
(663.63)

16. $\$0.45 + \$62.90 + \$23 = \underline{86.35}$

17. $50.1 + 652.12 + 3,067 + 0.88 = \underline{3770.70}$

```
   .45
 62.90
 23.00
------
 86.35
```

```
   50.1
  652.12
 3067.00
    .88
-------
 3770.10
```

MIXED APPLICATIONS

18. A tabletop is 4.717 centimeters thick. It is covered with a layer of 0.159 centimeter-thick laminated plastic. What is the total thickness?

```
 4.717
  .159
------
 4.876
```

$\underline{4.876\ centimeters\ thick}$

19. The monthly snowfall during the winter was 10.5 inches, 15.85 inches, and 8.6 inches. How much snow fell?

```
 10.5
 15.85
 8.6
-----
 34.95
```

$\underline{34.95\ inches\ of\ snow}$

20. In 1900, 4,192 cars were sold. In 1910, 181,000 cars were sold. How many more were sold in 1910 than 1900?

$\underline{176,808\ more\ cars}$

```
 181,000
 - 4,192
--------
 176,808
```

21. One year, Vermont had 378,000 licensed drivers and Wyoming had 365,000. Which state had the greater number of licensed drivers? By how many?

```
 378
 365
----
 013
```

$\underline{Vermont\ has\ more\ licensed}$
$\underline{drivers\ by\ 13,000\ drivers.}$

NUMBER SENSE

22. How is 2.36 different from 23.6? Is the sum $2.36 + 9.8$ the same as the sum $23.6 + 9.8$? Explain.

$\underline{2.36\ is\ different\ because\ 23.6\ is\ 23\ wholes\ and\ 6\ tenths\ 2.36}$
$\underline{is\ 2\ wholes\ and\ 3\ tents\ and\ 6\ hundreths\ No\ because\ 2.36}$
$\underline{is\ less\ than\ 23.6.}$

Unit 2
Core Skills Math, Grade 6

Subtracting Decimals

Place the decimal point in each difference.

1. $7.46 - 2.84 = 4.62$

2. $17.17 - 5.7 = 11.47$

3. $29.009 - 0.25 = 28.759$

Find each difference.

4. $9.8 - 3.95 = \underline{5.85}$

5. $39.32 - 12.6 = \underline{26.72}$

6. $239.8 - 73.91 = \underline{165.89}$

7. $96.111 - 7.02 = \underline{89.091}$

8. $1.009 - 0.83 = \underline{.179}$

9. $5.53 - 4.888 = \underline{0.642}$

10. $7.27 - 3.621 = \underline{4.449}$

11. $15.13 - 5.2 = \underline{9.93}$

12. $17.3 - 2.519 = \underline{14.781}$

13. $26 - 12.274 = \underline{13.726}$

14. $6.036 - 4.71 = \underline{1.326}$

15. $0.38 - 0.175 = \underline{.205}$

16. $89.5 - 30.48 = \underline{59.02}$

17. $98 - 6.432 = \underline{91.568}$

18. $100.8 - 92.44 = \underline{8.36}$

19. $\begin{array}{r} 20.220 \\ -\ 2.555 \\ \hline 17.665 \end{array}$

20. $\begin{array}{r} 4.30 \\ -\ 0.99 \\ \hline 3.31 \end{array}$

21. $\begin{array}{r} 83.800 \\ -\ 0.765 \\ \hline 83.035 \end{array}$ 83.035

22. $\begin{array}{r} 78.30 \\ -\ 9.05 \\ \hline 69.25 \end{array}$ 69.25

23. $\begin{array}{r} 578.32 \\ -\ 17.69 \\ \hline 560.63 \end{array}$ 560.63

24. $\begin{array}{r} 57.0300 \\ -\ .0041 \\ \hline 57.0259 \end{array}$ 57.0259

MIXED APPLICATIONS

25. Martin ran a race in 38.65 seconds. Herb finished 1.8 seconds before Martin. How long did it take Herb to run the race?

   40.45 seconds.

26. Luisa has 5 yards of ribbon. She uses 2.25 yards on a dress and 1.6 yards on a blouse. How much ribbon does she have left?

   1.15 yards of ribbon

27. The LeMans 24-hour auto race covers 3,107.93 miles. Round the distance to the nearest 100 miles.

   about 3,100 miles

28. In 1906 the record speed for a car was 127.659 mph. In 1926 the record speed was 170.624 mph. About how much faster was the 1926 speed?

   57.035 mphs faster

NUMBER SENSE

29. Look at the problems $10.6 - 8.9$ and $106 - 89$. How are they similar? Which problem has a greater difference?

   106-89 does because they are farther apart they all use the same 4 digits

10

Name _____ Date _____

Adding and Subtracting Thousandths

Estimate each sum or difference to the nearest whole number.

1. 0.763
    + 0.922
    .200

2. 6.341
    − 3.462
    3.120

3. 24.913
    − 5.353
    19.640

4. 433.461
    + 76.980
    500.300

Find each sum or difference.

5. 18.012
    − 9.586

6. 2.017
    + 0.932

7. 16.000
    − 6.321

8. 432.036
    − 7.943

9. 32.980
    + 3.111

10. 334.999
     + 224.001

11. 1.000
     − 0.001

12. 531.005
     − 231.993

MIXED APPLICATIONS

13. Mrs. Chang used 45.332 gallons of gas in her car in September, 53.110 gallons in October, and 48.003 gallons in November. How much gas did she use in the three months combined?

_____

14. The price of gasoline at Al's Service Station is listed as $3.259. At A-One Gas it is listed at $3.199. At which station is gas less expensive? How much would you save if you bought one gallon of the less expensive gas?

_____

SCIENCE CONNECTION

15. The body of a 150 lb man contains 3 lb calcium, 27 lb carbon, 0.31 lb chlorine, 15 lb hydrogen, 0.006 lb iron, 0.06 lb magnesium, 4.5 lb nitrogen, 97.5 lb oxygen, 1.8 lb phosphorous, 0.33 lb potassium, 0.165 lb sodium, 0.36 lb sulfur, and traces of other elements.

    Order the elements in a table, from least to greatest, according to weight.

11

Multiplying Decimals

Place the decimal point in each product.

1. $6.8 \times 3.4 = 2\ 3\ 1\ 2$ **2.** $2.56 \times 4.6 = 1\ 1\ 7\ 7\ 6$

3. $6.787 \times 7.6 = 5\ 1\ 5\ 8\ 1\ 2$ **4.** $0.98 \times 4.6 = 4\ 5\ 0\ 8$

5. $0.97 \times 0.76 = 0\ 7\ 3\ 7\ 2$ **6.** $3.761 \times 0.5 = 1\ 8\ 8\ 0\ 5$

7.
$$\begin{array}{r} 34.45 \\ \times\ \ 3.3 \\ \hline 1\ 1\ 3\ 6\ 8\ 5 \end{array}$$
8.
$$\begin{array}{r} 69 \\ \times\ 4.7 \\ \hline 3\ 2\ 4\ 3 \end{array}$$
9.
$$\begin{array}{r} 4.343 \\ \times\ \ 0.8 \\ \hline 3\ 4\ 7\ 4\ 4 \end{array}$$
10.
$$\begin{array}{r} 78.3 \\ \times\ 234 \\ \hline 1\ 8\ 3\ 2\ 2\ 2 \end{array}$$

Find each product. Round money amounts to the nearest cent.

11.
$$\begin{array}{r} 6.8 \\ \times\ 3.4 \\ \hline \end{array}$$
12.
$$\begin{array}{r} 4.435 \\ \times\ \ 5.6 \\ \hline \end{array}$$
13.
$$\begin{array}{r} 456.2 \\ \times\ \ \ 3.5 \\ \hline \end{array}$$
14.
$$\begin{array}{r} \$25.98 \\ \times\ \ \ \ 6.7 \\ \hline \end{array}$$
15.
$$\begin{array}{r} 35.9 \\ \times\ 0.08 \\ \hline \end{array}$$

16.
$$\begin{array}{r} 68.77 \\ \times\ \ \ 28 \\ \hline \end{array}$$
17.
$$\begin{array}{r} \$14.87 \\ \times\ \ \ \ 0.9 \\ \hline \end{array}$$
18.
$$\begin{array}{r} \$674.65 \\ \times\ \ \ \ \ 9.4 \\ \hline \end{array}$$
19.
$$\begin{array}{r} \$523.78 \\ \times\ \ \ \ \ 0.5 \\ \hline \end{array}$$
20.
$$\begin{array}{r} 0.89 \\ \times\ 0.6 \\ \hline \end{array}$$

21. $15.8 \times 54 =$ _____   **22.** $\$125.65 \times 3.7 =$ _____   **23.** $6.89 \times 45 =$ _____

24. $543.2 \times 0.25 =$ _____   **25.** $7,965 \times 4.315 =$ _____   **26.** $1.5 \times 0.065 =$ _____

MIXED APPLICATIONS

27. Marilyn bought cotton that sells for $2.35 a yard. To the nearest cent, how much will she pay for 3.5 yards of cotton?

_____

28. León makes $8.35 an hour. About how much did he make last week if he worked 39.5 hours?

_____

NUMBER SENSE

29. Look at the problems 2.3×3.68 and 23×368. How are they similar? Which problem has the greater product?

_____

_____

Name _____ Date _____

Zeros in the Product

Place the decimal point in the product. Write zeros where necessary.

1. 0.02
    × 3.6
    ———
    7 2

2. 0.003
    × 22.7
    ———
    6 8 1

3. 0.098
    × 4.1
    ———
    4 0 1 8

4. 1.98
    × 0.5
    ———
    9 9 0

5. 0.0004
    ×   35
    ———
    1 4 0

Find each product.

6. 0.078
    ×   9

7. 45.99
    × 20.6

8. 0.07
    × 6

9. 34.79
    × 0.05

10. 0.67
    × 507

11. 0.098
    × 0.6

12. 0.0045
    × 669

13. 8.7
    × 0.6

14. 0.37
    × 3.78

15. 0.002
    × 60.4

16. 6.213
    × 19

17. 29.1
    × 0.02

18. 0.06
    × 0.21

19. 3.44
    × 0.22

20. 0.072
    ×   6

21. $5.7 \times 100 =$ _____

22. $0.081 \times 10 =$ _____

23. $0.086 \times 1{,}000 =$ _____

24. $0.956 \times 100 =$ _____

25. $17.8 \times 1{,}000 =$ _____

26. $456.9 \times 10 =$ _____

MIXED APPLICATIONS

27. A modern art poster is 0.0048 centimeter thick. How thick is a stack of 6 modern art posters?

    _____

28. Cheese costs $3.99 a pound. To the nearest cent, how much will 2.05 pounds cost?

    _____

NUMBER SENSE

29. Look at the problems 0.06×2.49 and 0.6×2.49. How are they similar? Which problem has the greater product?

_____

_____

13

Dividing Decimals by Whole Numbers

Find each quotient.

1. $4\overline{)12.8}$ _____

2. $8\overline{)13.76}$ _____

3. $7\overline{)26.6}$ _____

4. $50.4 \div 12 =$ _____

Place the decimal point in each quotient.

5. $30.16 \div 13 = 2\ 3\ 2$

6. $2.08 \div 8 = 0\ 2\ 6$

7. $86.4 \div 27 = 3\ 2$

Find each quotient.

8. $6\overline{)14.76}$ _____

9. $11\overline{)11.88}$ _____

10. $4\overline{)2.184}$ _____

11. $13\overline{)66.3}$ _____

12. $9\overline{)4.158}$ _____

13. $5\overline{)13.5}$ _____

14. $8\overline{)68.16}$ _____

15. $29\overline{)152.25}$ _____

16. $3.478 \div 74 =$ ____

17. $47.61 \div 23 =$ ____

18. $44.24 \div 7 =$ ____

19. $263.5 \div 5 =$ ____

MIXED APPLICATIONS

20. There are 25 students in Angela's aerobics class. Angela collected $67.55 in class fees from each student. What is the total amount that Angela collected?

    _____

21. The total weight of 5 apples is 3.75 pounds. If each apple weighs about the same, about how much does each apple weigh?

    _____

EVERYDAY MATH CONNECTIONS

22. A crafts store sells two brands of embroidery floss. Brand A costs $2.64 for 12 skeins. Brand B sells for $0.28 a skein. Which brand is a better buy?

    _____

Dividing Decimals with Zeros in the Dividend

Divide until each remainder is zero.

1. $6\overline{)77.1}$ _____

2. $8\overline{)20.76}$ _____

3. $4\overline{)33.7}$ _____

4. $8\overline{)5.2}$ _____

5. $4\overline{)28.7}$ _____

6. $5\overline{)1.58}$ _____

7. $12\overline{)71.4}$ _____

8. $28\overline{)207.34}$ _____

9. $16\overline{)59.6}$ _____

10. $24\overline{)12.12}$ _____

11. $35\overline{)15.12}$ _____

12. $68\overline{)242.76}$ _____

13. $8.6 \div 40 =$ _____

14. $2.92 \div 8 =$ _____

15. $6.276 \div 6 =$ _____

16. $27.36 \div 60 =$ _____

MIXED APPLICATIONS

17. Louise can run 4 miles in 21 minutes. How long does it take her to run 1 mile?

_____

18. The cost of 1 ticket to a basketball game is $6.50. What is the cost of 8 tickets?

_____

LOGICAL REASONING

Mr. Martin owns a grocery store. A case of 48 cans of dog food costs him $21.60.

19. How much does Mr. Martin pay for each can of dog food?

_____

20. Suppose that Mr. Martin sells each can for $0.10 more than he paid. What is the selling price of each can?

_____

Exploring Dividing Decimals by Decimals

Use a calculator to examine what happens to the quotient when you multiply each divisor and each dividend by the same power of ten.

1. **A.** Multiply both 4.8 and 1.2 by 10. _____

   B. Divide 48 by 12. _____

   C. Now multiply both 4.8 and 1.2 by 100. _____

   D. Divide 480 by 120. _____

   E. How do the quotients of 48 ÷ 12 and 480 ÷ 120 compare with that of 4.8 ÷ 1.2?

   _____

2. How does multiplying the divisor and the dividend by the same power of 10 affect the quotient?

   _____

Find each quotient.

3. 8.8 ÷ 4.4 = _____   4. 6.6 ÷ 1.1 = _____   5. 9.9 ÷ 3.3 = _____

6. 7.8 ÷ 2.6 = _____   7. 10.8 ÷ 5.4 = _____   8. 4.2 ÷ 2.1 = _____

Write whether the quotients will be the *same* or *different*.

9. 31.8 ÷ 4.2
   318 ÷ 42

   _____

10. 8.7 ÷ 2.01
    0.87 ÷ 0.0201

    _____

11. 520 ÷ 230
    5.2 ÷ 2.3

    _____

12. 23.4 ÷ 12.01
    234 ÷ 1,201

    _____

13. 1.04 ÷ 32.1
    10.4 ÷ 321

    _____

14. 0.63 ÷ 2.1
    6.3 ÷ 210

    _____

15. 4.56 ÷ 0.34
    456 ÷ 34

    _____

16. 6.07 ÷ 1.23
    6.07 ÷ 123

    _____

17. 12.9 ÷ 0.98
    129 ÷ 98

    _____

18. 8.88 ÷ 12.5
    8.88 ÷ 1.25

    _____

19. 722 ÷ 151
    72.2 ÷ 15.1

    _____

20. 621 ÷ 2.175
    .621 ÷ .02175

    _____

Name _____ Date _____

Dividing Decimals by Decimals

Place the decimal point in each quotient. Add zeros if necessary.

1. 32.85 ÷ 4.5 = 7   3

2. 2.08 ÷ 0.8 = 2   6

3. 368.48 ÷ 9.8 = 3   7   6

4. 0.115 ÷ 2.3 =   5

5. 39.52 ÷ 5.2 = 7   6

6. 27.307 ÷ 8.3 = 3   2   9

Find each quotient.

7. 2.38 ÷ 0.07 = _____

8. 89.6 ÷ 0.16 = _____

9. 0.2368 ÷ 0.37 = _____

10. 0.72)‾31.32 _____

11. 6.3)‾340.2 _____

12. 2.1)‾8.841 _____

13. 3.6)‾23.958 _____

14. 0.11)‾496.1 _____

15. 0.122)‾0.793 _____

16. 86.36 ÷ 34 = _____

17. 0.1449 ÷ 0.045 = _____

18. 58.42 ÷ 0.23 = _____

MIXED APPLICATIONS

19. Joanne earns $8.30 an hour. Last week she earned $306.27. For how many hours did she work?

_____

20. Eric bought 12.4 gallons of gasoline for $3.40 a gallon. How much did he pay for the gasoline?

_____

LOGICAL REASONING

21. Nan wants to rent a video game for $4.99. She has only dimes in her bank. How many dimes will she need to rent the game?

_____

More Decimal Division

Find each quotient.

1. $0.2\overline{)3.8}$ **2.** $0.5\overline{)7.5}$ **3.** $5.3\overline{)1.908}$ **4.** $0.008\overline{)0.472}$

5. $0.5\overline{)10.5}$ **6.** $1.3\overline{)2.86}$ **7.** $0.06\overline{)4.74}$ **8.** $2.05\overline{)12.505}$

Find each quotient to the nearest tenth.

9. $0.4\overline{)2.544}$ **10.** $0.06\overline{)1.4718}$ **11.** $0.174\overline{)3.286}$ **12.** $0.015\overline{)0.137}$

13. $0.8\overline{)1.925}$ **14.** $0.03\overline{)0.611}$ **15.** $1.06\overline{)4.012}$ **16.** $0.029\overline{)4.666}$

Find each quotient to the nearest hundredth.

17. $0.8\overline{)4.388}$ **18.** $0.24\overline{)1.64328}$ **19.** $7.4\overline{)0.477}$ **20.** $3.06\overline{)7}$

21. $1.7\overline{)0.923}$ **22.** $0.85\overline{)9.916}$ **23.** $1.02\overline{)26.14}$ **24.** $0.3\overline{)6.515}$

MIXED APPLICATIONS

25. The Bodacious Surfers Club bought 16 skimboards for $1,094.50. To the nearest cent, what was the average cost of each skimboard?

_____

26. Lucy earned $146.84 for one week of work as a lifeguard. Meg earned $734.20 as a model for a television commercial. How many times greater were Meg's earnings than Lucy's earnings?

_____

LOGICAL REASONING

27. Tom had $1.19 in coins. Vera asked him for change for a dollar, but he did not have the correct change. What coins could he have had?

_____

Recognize Statistical Questions

Identify the statistical question. Explain your reasoning.

1. **A.** How many touchdowns did the quarterback throw during the last game of the season?

   B. How many touchdowns did the quarterback throw each game of the season?

2. **A.** What was the score in the first frame of a bowling game?

   B. What are the scores in 10 frames of a bowling game?

3. **A.** How many hours of television did you watch each day this week?

   B. How many hours of television did you watch on Saturday?

Write a statistical question you could ask in the situation.

4. A teacher recorded the test scores of her students.

   _____

   _____

   _____

5. A car salesman knows how many of each model of a car was sold in a month.

   _____

   _____

   _____

MIXED APPLICATIONS

6. The city tracked the amount of waste that was recycled from 2009 to 2012. Write a statistical question about the situation.

   _____

   _____

   _____

7. The daily low temperature is recorded for a week. Write a statistical question about the situation.

   _____

   _____

   _____

Describe Distributions

Chase asked people how many songs they have bought online in the past month. Use the histogram of the data he collected for 1–4.

1. What statistical question could Chase ask about the data?

   _____

   _____

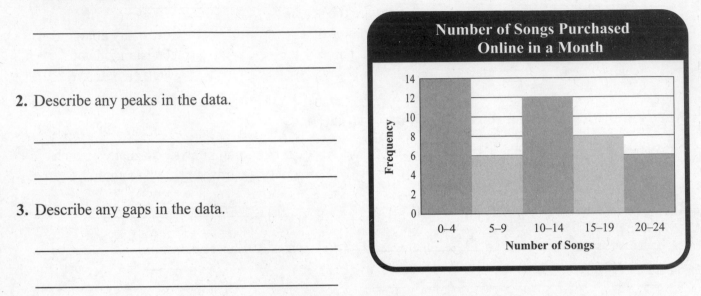

2. Describe any peaks in the data.

   _____

   _____

3. Describe any gaps in the data.

   _____

   _____

4. Does the graph have symmetry? Explain your reasoning.

   _____

   _____

MIXED APPLICATIONS

5. Mr. Carpenter teaches five classes each day. For several days in a row, he kept track of the number of students who were late to class and displayed the results in a dot plot. Describe the data.

   _____

   _____

   _____

   _____

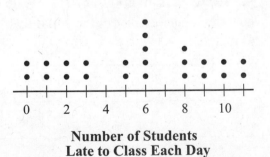

Number of Students
Late to Class Each Day

Relating Bar Graphs and Histograms

Tell whether a bar graph or a histogram is more appropriate for Exercises 1–2. Explain your answer.

1. Charlotte is collecting data about the number of girls enrolled at the Central Gymnastics School.

_____

_____

_____

2. Timothy is collecting data about the number of people at the mall from noon to 5:00 P.M.

_____

_____

_____

3. Use the data to make a bar graph on a separate sheet of paper.

Favorite Car	
Make of Car	**Votes**
Ford	21
Chevrolet	15
Kia	24
Toyota	12
Nissan	10

4. Use the data to make a histogram on a separate sheet of paper.

Test Scores	Frequency
61–65	3
66–70	8
71–75	6
76–80	6
81–85	5
86–90	4
91–95	2
96 100	1

MIXED APPLICATIONS

5. Describe the type of data for which you could draw a bar graph. Why is a bar graph a good way to graph this type of data?

_____

6. Describe the type of data for which you could draw a histogram. Why is a histogram a good way to graph this type of data?

_____

WRITER'S CORNER

7. Write a problem that can be solved using the data from Exercise 3.

_____

_____

Exploring Averages

Ana's Photographs	
Zoo	9
Family Picnic	6
Space Museum	7
Birthday Party	10
School Play	3

Imagine using cubes to explore finding the average. The data in the table tell how many photographs from several places Ana took. Let one cube stand for one photograph.

Use the table for Exercises 1–5.

1. If you made one stack for each location in the table, how many stacks would you make?

   _____

2. Write a number sentence to show how many cubes you used in all?

   _____

3. Arrange the cubes in five equal stacks. How many cubes are in each stack?

   _____

4. What is the average number of photographs that Ana took of each place?

   _____

5. Write a number sentence to show how you found your answer.

   _____

SCIENCE CONNECTION

6. Three crews worked in a space station. They spent 29, 58, and 84 days in the space station. What was the mean length of time the crews spent in the station? Write two number sentences, one addition and one division, to show how you got the answer.

   _____

Core Skills Math, Grade 6

Median, Range, and Mean

Find the median, range, and mean for each set of numbers.

1. 3, 10, 5 _____

2. 22, 42, 35 _____

3. 4, 11, 9, 6, 5 _____

4. 35, 26, 18, 25, 31 _____

5. 112, 64, 67, 79, 103 _____

6. 96, 120, 102, 95, 124, 101, 125 _____

Find the mean for each set of test scores.

7. 83, 97, 100, 84, 76 _____

8. 89, 92, 75, 100, 98, 92 _____

MIXED APPLICATIONS

9. Find the median, range, and mean of the data in the graph.

_____

Types of Computer Software in School						
Writing	15					
Math	23					
Graphics	7					
Science	11					
Games	4					
	0 5 10 15 20 25 30					

SOCIAL STUDIES CONNECTION

10. Imagine that you work as a survey taker. Collect data by asking 5 to 9 people this question: About how many hours of television do you watch in one week? Record your results in the chart.

Hours of TV Watched in One Week								
Names								
Hours								

Find the median, range, and mean number of hours of television watched in one week.

_____

23

Range, Mean, Median, and Mode

Complete the table.

	Data	Range	Mean	Median	Mode
1.	37, 36, 76, 84, 37				
2.	87, 98, 91, 75, 89				
3.	68, 85, 70, 57, 88, 88				
4.	96, 85, 52, 84, 85, 83, 40				
5.	90, 94, 65, 90, 84, 94, 85				
6.	82, 56, 46, 67, 89, 97, 56, 67				

MIXED APPLICATIONS

7. The test scores for the last test in Mrs. Kwan's class were 84, 73, 91, 60, 76, 78, 74, 79, 76, and 89. What is the mean of the scores? What is the range of the scores?

_____

8. The student who earned a 60 on the test transferred to another class. If Mrs. Kwan drops the 60, what is the mean of the remaining scores? What is the range?

_____

MIXED REVIEW

Place the decimal point in each product.

9. $6.38 \times 33 = 2\ 1\ 0\ 5\ 4$

10. $46.71 \times 2.5 = 1\ 1\ 6\ 7\ 7\ 5$

11. $2.94 \times 9 = 2\ 6\ 4\ 6$

12. $15.76 \times .03 = 0\ 4\ 7\ 2\ 8$

Place the decimal point in each quotient.

13. $8.99 \div 0.62 = 0\ 1\ 4\ 5$

14. $21.05 \div 0.2 = 1\ 0\ 5\ 2\ 5$

15. $272.335 \div 2.17 = 1\ 2\ 5\ 5\ 0$

16. $18.62 \div 0.02 = 9\ 3\ 1\ 0$

Find each quotient.

17. $2.17\overline{)18.228}$ _____

18. $0.21\overline{)1.3545}$ _____

Misleading Statistics

Mr. Jackson wants to make dinner reservations at a restaurant that has most meals costing less than $16. The Waterside Inn advertises that they have meals that average $15. The table shows the menu items.

Menu Items	
Meal	**Price**
Potato Soup	$6
Chicken	$16
Steak	$18
Pasta	$16
Shrimp	$18
Crab Cake	$19

1. What is the minimum price and maximum price?

min = _____

max = _____

2. What is the mean of the prices?

_____

3. Construct a box plot for the data.

4. What is the range of the prices?

_____

5. What is the median of the prices?

_____

6. What is the interquartile range of the prices?

_____

7. Does the menu match Mr. Jackson's requirements? Explain your reasoning.

_____

_____

_____

Apply Measures of Center and Variability

1. The table shows temperature data for two cities. Use the information in the table to compare the data.

   The mean of City 1's temperatures is _____ the mean of City 2's temperatures.

   The _____ of City 1's temperatures is

   _____ the _____ of City 2's temperatures.

   So, City 2 is typically _____ City 1, and City 2's

   temperatures vary _____ City 1's temperatures.

Daily High Temperatures (°F)		
	Mean	Interquartile Range
City 1	60	7
City 2	70	15

2. The table shows weights of fish that were caught in two different lakes. Find the median and range of each data set and use these measures to compare the data.

Fish Weight (pounds)
Lake A: 7, 9, 10, 4, 6, 12
Lake B: 6, 7, 4, 5, 6, 4

MIXED APPLICATIONS

3. Mrs. Mack measured the heights of her students in two classes. Class 1 has a mean height of 130 cm and an interquartile range of 5 cm. Class 2 has a mean height of 134 cm and an interquartile range of 8 cm. Write a statement that compares the data.

   _____

   _____

   _____

4. Richard's science test scores are 76, 80, 78, 84, and 80. His math test scores are 100, 80, 73, 94, and 71. Compare the medians and interquartile ranges.

   _____

   _____

   _____

Dot Plots and Frequency Tables

Use the chart to complete Exercises 1–4.

1. The chart shows the number of pages of a novel that Julia reads each day. Complete the dot plot using the data in the table.

Pages Read				
12	14	12	18	20
15	15	19	12	15
14	11	13	18	15
15	17	12	11	15

Pages Read

2. What number of pages does Julia read most often? Explain.

_____

_____

3. Make a frequency table in the space below. Use the intervals 10–13, 14–17, and 18–21.

4. Make a relative frequency table in the space below.

MIXED APPLICATIONS

5. The frequency table shows the ages of the actors in a youth theater group. What percent of the actors are 10 to 12 years old?

Actors in a Youth Theater Group	
Age	Frequency
7–9	8
10–12	22
13–15	10

Name _____ Date _____

Box Plots

Find the median, lower quartile, and upper quartile of the data in Exercises 1 and 2.

1. the amounts of juice in 12 glasses, in fluid ounces:

    11, 8, 4, 9, 12, 14, 9, 16, 15, 11, 10, 7

    Order the data from least to greatest: 4, 7, 8, 9, 9, 10, 11, 11, 12, 14, 15, 16

    median: _____   lower quartile: _____   upper quartile: _____

2. the lengths of 10 pencils, in centimeters:

    18, 15, 4, 9, 14, 17, 16, 6, 8, 10

    median: _____   lower quartile: _____   upper quartile: _____

3. Make a box plot to display the data set in Exercise 2.

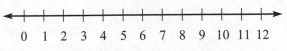

Lengths of Pencils (centimeters)

4. The numbers of students on several teams are 9, 4, 5, 10, 11, 9, 8, and 6. Make a box plot for the data.

```
    ←—+—+—+—+—+—+—+—+—+—+—+—+—→
      0  1  2  3  4  5  6  7  8  9 10 11 12
```

Number of Students on a Team

MIXED APPLICATIONS

5. The amounts spent at a gift shop today are $19, $30, $28, $22, $20, $26, and $26. What is the median? What is the lower quartile?

    _____

6. The weights of six puppies in ounces are 8, 5, 7, 5, 6, and 9. What is the upper quartile of the data?

    _____

Describe Data Collection

Describe the data set by listing the attribute measured, the unit of measure, the likely means of measurement, and the number of observations.

1. Daily temperature

Daily High Temperature (°F)				
78	83	72	65	70
76	75	71	80	75
73	74	81	79	69
81	78	76	80	82
70	77	74	71	73

_____

_____

_____

2. Plant heights

Height of Plants (inches)				
10.3	9.7	6.4	8.1	11.2
5.7	11.7	7.5	9.6	6.9

_____

_____

_____

3. Cereal in boxes

Amount of Cereal in Boxes (cups)							
8	7	8.5	5	5	5	6.5	6
8	8.5	7	7	9	8	8	9

_____

_____

_____

4. Dog weights

Weight of Dogs (pounds)							
22	17	34	23	19	18	20	20

_____

_____

_____

MIXED APPLICATIONS

5. The table below gives the amount of time Preston spends on homework. Name the likely means of measurement.

Amount of Time Spent on Homework (hours)							
5	3	1	2	4	1	3	2

_____

6. The table below shows the speed of cars on a highway. Name the unit of measure.

Speeds of Cars (miles per hour)							
71	55	53	65	68	61	59	62
70	69	57	50	56	66	67	63

_____

Patterns in Data

1. The dot plot shows the number of omelets ordered at Paul's Restaurant each day. Does the dot plot contain any gaps?

   _____

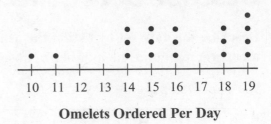

Omelets Ordered Per Day

2. Identify any clusters in the data.

   _____

   _____

3. Summarize the information in the dot plot.

   _____

   _____

   _____

Use the histogram to answer Exercises 4–5.

4. The histogram shows the number of people that visited a local shop each day in January. How many peaks does the histogram have?

   _____

5. Describe how the data values change across the intervals.

   _____

   _____

   _____

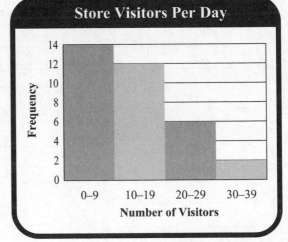

MIXED APPLICATIONS

6. Look at the dot plot at the right. Does the graph have line symmetry? Explain.

   _____

   _____

   _____

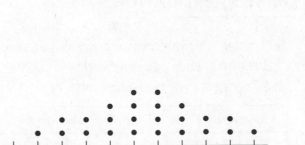

Gift Cards Purchased This Week

30

Name _____ Date _____

Mean Absolute Deviation

Find the mean absolute deviation of the data.

1. the number of hours Maggie spent practicing soccer for 4 different weeks:

   9, 6, 6, 7
   mean = 7 hours
   $|9 - 7| = 2$
   $|6 - 7| = 1$
   $|6 - 7| = 1$
   $|7 - 7| = 0$

   $\dfrac{(2 + 1 + 1 + 0)}{4} = 1$

   mean absolute deviation = _____

2. the heights of 7 people in inches:

   60, 64, 58, 60, 70, 71, 65

   mean = 64 inches

   mean absolute deviation = _____

Use the dot plot to find the mean absolute deviation of the data.

3. mean = 10

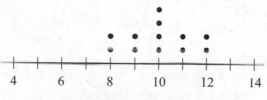

Ages of Students in Dance Class

mean absolute deviation = _____

4. mean = 8

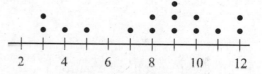

Weekly Hours Spent Doing Homework

mean absolute deviation = _____

MIXED APPLICATIONS

5. In science class, Troy found the mass, in grams, of 6 samples to be 10, 12, 7, 8, 5, and 6. What is the mean absolute deviation?

6. Five recorded temperatures are 71°F, 64°F, 72°F, 81°F, and 67°F. What is the mean absolute deviation?

_____   _____

Measures of Variability

Find the range and interquartile range of the data in the box plot.

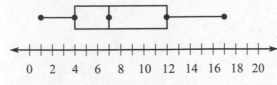

Miles Walked

1. For the range, find the difference between the greatest and least values.

   _____ – _____ = _____

   range: _____

2. For the interquartile range, find the difference between the upper and lower quartiles.

   _____ – _____ = _____

   interquartile range: _____

Use the box plot to answer Exercises 2-3.

3. What is the range of the data?

   _____

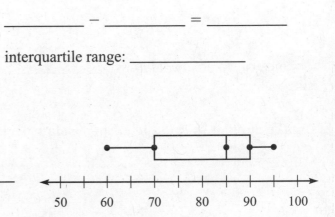

Quiz Scores

4. What is the interquartile range of the data?

   _____

5. Find the mean absolute deviation for the data giving the heights in centimeters of several flowers:

   14, 7, 6, 5, 13

   mean absolute deviation: _____.

6. Find the mean absolute deviation for the data giving the ages of several children:

   5, 7, 4, 6, 3, 5, 3, 7

   mean absolute deviation: _____

MIXED APPLICATIONS

7. The following data set gives the amount of time, in minutes, it took five people to cook a recipe. What is the mean absolute deviation for the data?

   33, 38, 31, 36, 37

   _____

8. The prices of six food processors are $63, $59, $72, $68, $61, and $67. What is the mean absolute deviation for the data?

   _____

Effects of Outliers

1. Identify the outlier in the data set of students in each class. Then describe the effect the outlier has on the mean and median.

Students in Each Class				
30	22	26	21	24
28	23	26	28	12

_____

_____

2. Identify the outlier in the data set of pledge amounts. Then describe the effect the outlier has on the mean and median.

Pledge Amounts			
$100	$10	$15	$20
$17	$24	$32	$36

_____

_____

3. In a set of points that Milton scored in basketball games, there is an outlier. Before one game, Milton injured his knee. Do you think the outlier is greater or less than the rest of the numbers of points? Explain.

_____

_____

MIXED APPLICATIONS

4. Duke's science quiz scores are 99, 91, 60, 94, and 95. Describe the effect of the outlier on the mean and median.

_____

_____

5. The number of people who attended an art conference for five days was 42, 27, 35, 39, and 96. Describe the effect of the outlier on the mean and median.

_____

_____

_____

33

Choose Appropriate Measures of Center and Variability

1. The distances, in miles, that 6 people travel to get to work are 14, 12, 2, 16, 16, and 18. Decide which measure(s) of center best describes the data set. Explain your reasoning.

The _____ is less than 4 of the data points, and the _____ describes only 2 of the data points. So, the _____ best describes the data.

mean = _____

median = _____

mode = _____

2. The numbers of pets that several children have are 2, 1, 2, 3, 4, 3, 10, 0, 1, and 0. Make a box plot of the data and find the range and interquartile range. Decide which measure better describes the data set and explain your reasoning.

```
<---+--+--+--+--+--+--+--+--+--+--+--+-->
    0  1  2  3  4  5  6  7  8  9  10 11 12
```

range = _____

interquartile range = _____

_____

_____

_____

MIXED APPLICATIONS

3. Brett's history quiz scores are 84, 78, 92, 90, 85, 91, and 0. Decide which measure(s) of center best describes the data set. Explain your reasoning.

mean = _____ median = _____

mode = _____

_____

_____

_____

4. Eight students were absent the following number of days in a year: 4, 8, 0, 1, 7, 2, 6, and 3. Decide if the range or interquartile range better describes the data set and explain your reasoning.

range = _____

interquartile range = _____

_____

_____

_____

Powers and Exponents

Write in exponent form.

1. five squared _____

2. eight to the 5th power _____

3. nine cubed _____

4. $2 \times 2 \times 2 \times 2$ _____

5. $7 \times 7 \times 7 \times 7 \times 7 \times 7$ _____

6. 2.3×2.3 _____

Find each value.

7. 5^4 _____

8. thirteen squared _____

9. $(1.2)^2$ _____

10. 18^0 _____

11. one thousand squared _____

12. $7^2 \times 7^0$ _____

MIXED APPLICATIONS

13. Mai bought a new car. She drove 6^3 miles the first month and 6^4 miles the second month. How much farther did she drive the second month?

_____

_____

_____

14. Mai bought gasoline at $3.39 per gallon. She paid $50.85. How many gallons did she buy?

_____

_____

MIXED REVIEW

Estimate each product or quotient.

15. 23.9×4.3 _____

16. $73.1 \div 9.2$ _____

17. 6×19.98 _____

18. $289.3 \div 7.25$ _____

Find each product or quotient.

19. $3,052 \times 44$ _____

20. $5,280 \div 30$ _____

21. 6.9×1.5 _____

22. $90 \div 1.2$ _____

Exponents and Place Value

Complete the place-value chart.

Power of 20	Millions			Thousands			Ones		
	Hundreds	Tens	Ones	Hundreds	Tens	Ones	Hundreds	Tens	Ones
1. 20^1								□	□
2. □							4	0	0
3. □						8,	0	0	0
4. 20^4				□	□	□,	□	□	□
5. 20^5			□,	□	□	□,	□	□	□

Tell how many zeros will be in each number when written in standard form.

6. 10^3 _____ 7. ten squared _____

8. 10^{12} _____ 9. 10^{25} _____

10. ten to the fifth power _____ 11. 10^{33} _____

Write each number in standard form.

12. 10^7 _____ 13 10^4 _____ 14. $10 \times 10 \times 10$ _____

LOGICAL THINKING

15. A googolplex is 10 to the power of a googol, or $10^{10^{100}}$.
    How many zeros are in a googolplex?
    Hint: Think in terms of googols of zeros.

Name _____ Date _____

Factors, Primes, and Composites

Tell whether each number is _prime_ or _composite_.

1. 13 _____   **2.** 18 _____   **3.** 31 _____   **4.** 32 _____

5. 45 _____   **6.** 53 _____   **7.** 72 _____   **8.** 81 _____

Write the factors of each number.

9. 8 _____   **10.** 15 _____   **11.** 10 _____

12. 24 _____   **13.** 35 _____   **14.** 28 _____

_____

15. 100 _____   **16.** 65 _____   **17.** 50 _____

_____

18. 34 _____   **19.** 40 _____   **20.** 77 _____

_____

21. 84 _____   **22.** 45 _____   **23.** 46 _____

_____

MIXED APPLICATIONS

24. The sum of two numbers is 12. One number is prime and the other number is composite. What are the numbers?

_____

25. Danny has 48 flowers to plant in his garden. If each row in his garden must have the same number of flowers, what different arrangements can Danny make?

_____

_____

NUMBER SENSE

26. Name the greatest prime number less than 50.

_____

27. Name the least prime number greater than 50.

_____

Primes and Composites

Tell whether each number is *prime* or *composite*.

1. 3 _____   2. 5 _____   3. 86 _____

4. 89 _____   5. 93 _____   6. 51 _____

Write the prime factorization of each number using exponents.

7. 18 _____   8. 34 _____   9. 48 _____

10. 56 _____   11. 16 _____   12. 72 _____

13. 54 _____   14. 58 _____   15. 60 _____

16. 100 _____   17. 140 _____   18. 200 _____

Write the number represented by each prime factorization.

19. 2×3^2 _____   20. $3^2 \times 5 \times 7$ _____   21. $2^3 \times 5^2 \times 11$ _____

22. $3 \times 5 \times 7^2$ _____   23. $5^2 \times 7 \times 11$ _____   24. $2^2 \times 19$ _____

25. $2^3 \times 3^2$ _____   26. $3^3 \times 7 \times 11$ _____   27. $2^4 \times 5 \times 13$ _____

MIXED APPLICATIONS

28. Max has 36 tiles to use for a rectangular design. How many choices for the shape of the design does he have?

_____

29. The sum of two consecutive prime numbers is 52. Their difference is 6. Find the prime numbers.

_____

NUMBER SENSE

30. Which whole numbers less than 50 have prime factorizations composed of a prime number squared?

_____

38

Using a Factor Tree

Use a factor tree to find the prime factorization of each number in Exercises 1–6. The first one is done for you.

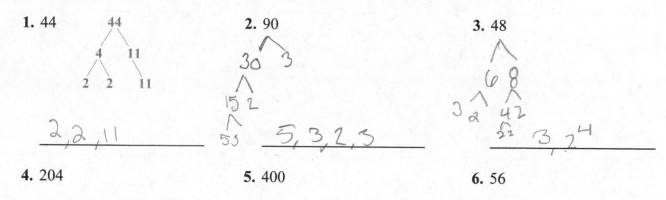

1. 44

        44
    4   11
  2 2   11

__2, 2, 11__

2. 90

__5, 3, 2, 3__

3. 48

__3, 2⁴__

4. 204

5. 400

6. 56

For Exercises 7–9, write the number whose prime factorization is given.

7. $3 \times 3 \times 11$

8. $2 \times 2 \times 7 \times 13$

9. $2 \times 3 \times 3 \times 3$

<hr>

MIXED APPLICATIONS

10. A computer code is based on the prime factorization of 160. Find the prime factorization of 160.

11. The combination for a lock is a 3-digit number. The digits are the prime factors of 42 listed from least to greatest. What is the combination for the lock?

Prime Factorization

Use a factor tree. Write the prime factorization of each number.

1. 20 _____   **2.** 75 _____   **3.** 63 _____

4. 56 _____   **5.** 18 _____   **6.** 54 _____

Write each prime factorization in exponent form.

7. 16 _____   **8.** 24 _____   **9.** 28 _____

10. 45 _____   **11.** 40 _____   **12.** 36 _____

MIXED APPLICATIONS

13. If $\frac{1}{4}$ of a group of students have math homework and $\frac{1}{5}$ have science homework, what is the least number of students in the group?

_____

14. A number f is a prime factor both of 12 and 21. What is f?

_____

MATH CONNECTION

15. What is the LCM (least common multiple) of a pair of numbers whose prime factorizations are $2^2 \times 3 \times 5$ and 2×3^2?

_____

16. The LCM of a pair of numbers is 60. The prime factorization of one number is 3×5. What is the prime factorization of the other number?

_____

Exploring Common Factors

List the factors of each number.

1. 14

2. 12

3. 13

4. 24

_____

_____

_____

_____

_____

_____

_____

_____

5. 36

6. 32

7. 64

8. 91

_____

_____

_____

_____

_____

_____

_____

_____

List the factors of each number. Write the common factors for each pair of numbers.

9. 8, 16

10. 9, 24

11. 10, 15

12. 12, 13

8: _____

9: _____

10: _____

12: _____

16: _____

24: _____

15: _____

_____

_____

_____

_____

13: _____

_____

_____

_____

_____

List the factors of each number. Write the greatest common factor for each pair of numbers.

13. 9, 27

14. 12, 18

15. 13, 39

16. 14, 21

_____

_____

_____

_____

_____

_____

_____

_____

_____

_____

_____

_____

LOGICAL THINKING

Write all the common factors for each pair of numbers.

17. 7, 13 _____

18. 5, 19 _____

19. 23, 31 _____

20. 11, 41 _____

21. Name two ways in which problems 17–20 are alike.

_____

_____

41

Greatest Common Factor

Write the common factors of each pair of numbers.

1. 16, 30 _____

2. 12, 18 _____

3. 24, 30 _____

4. 15, 45 _____

5. 20, 30 _____

6. 15, 20 _____

Write the GCF of each pair of numbers.

7. 8, 10 _____

8. 16, 18 _____

9. 7, 21 _____

10. 54, 9 _____

11. 15, 20 _____

12. 12, 8 _____

13. 15, 45 _____

14. 48, 6 _____

15. 30, 24 _____

16. 9, 21 _____

17. 12, 15 _____

18. 18, 36 _____

MIXED APPLICATIONS

19. Samantha has two pieces of cloth. One piece is 72 inches wide and the other piece is 90 inches wide. She wants to cut both pieces into strips of equal width that are as wide as possible. How wide should she cut the strips?

_____

20. Mrs. Rodriguez used $\frac{3}{4}$ yard of fabric to make an apron. She used $\frac{2}{3}$ yard to make place mats. Did she use more fabric to make the apron or the place mats?

_____

MIXED REVIEW

Write the equivalent fractions.

21. $\frac{2}{3} = \frac{\boxed{}}{9}$

22. $\frac{1}{5} = \frac{\boxed{}}{10}$

23. $\frac{6}{12} = \frac{1}{\boxed{}}$

24. $\frac{3}{8} = \frac{12}{\boxed{}}$

25. $\frac{2}{7} = \frac{14}{\boxed{}}$

Write in order from greatest to least. Use >.

26. $\frac{2}{7}, \frac{3}{7}, \frac{1}{7}$

27. $\frac{4}{5}, \frac{1}{2}, \frac{2}{3}$

28. $\frac{1}{8}, \frac{3}{12}, \frac{1}{6}$

_____   _____   _____

Write the factors of each number.

29. 8 _____

30. 28 _____

31. 54 _____

42

Multiples and Least Common Multiple

Write the first three multiples of each number, excluding the number itself.

1. 4　　　　　**2.** 8　　　　　**3.** 10　　　　　**4.** 3　　　　　**5.** 5

_____　　_____　　_____　　_____　　_____

6. 7　　　　　**7.** 11　　　　　**8.** 6　　　　　**9.** 9　　　　　**10.** 12

_____　　_____　　_____　　_____　　_____

Find the LCM for each group of numbers.

11. 8, 10　　**12.** 2, 12　　**13.** 4, 7　　**14.** 7, 9　　**15.** 6, 10

_____　　_____　　_____　　_____　　_____

16. 3, 8　　**17.** 7, 12　　**18.** 5, 8　　**19.** 3, 7　　**20.** 5, 7

_____　　_____　　_____　　_____　　_____

21. 2, 3　　**22.** 3, 4　　**23.** 8, 12　　**24.** 6, 9　　**25.** 3, 9

_____　　_____　　_____　　_____　　_____

MIXED APPLICATIONS

26. One model train can complete its track in 2 minutes. The other model train takes 3 minutes. If the two trains start at the same time, when will they both be at the starting point of their tracks at the same time?

_____

27. Donald wants to buy the same number of apples and pears. Apples are sold in packages of 4 and pears are sold in packages of 7. What is the least number of apples he can buy?

_____

LOGICAL REASONING

28. The LCM of a pair of numbers is 12. The sum of the numbers is 10. What are the numbers?

_____

29. The LCM of a pair of numbers is 8. The difference between the numbers is 6. What are the numbers?

_____

Exploring Least Common Denominator

1. Find common multiples

   of 4 and 6. _____

   What are two common denominators for $\frac{1}{4}$ and $\frac{5}{6}$? _____

   4: 4, 8, 12, 16, 20, 24

   6: 6, 12, 18, 24, 30, 36

2. Find common multiples

   of 2 and 4. _____

   What are two common denominators for $\frac{1}{2}$ and $\frac{1}{4}$? _____

   2: 2, 4, 6, 8, 10

   4: 4, 8, 12, 16, 20

3. Find common multiples

   of 5 and 10. _____

   What are two common denominators for $\frac{2}{5}$ and $\frac{3}{10}$? _____

   5: 5, 10, 15, 20, 25

   10: 10, 20, 30, 40, 50

Write each pair of fractions by using the LCD.

4. $\frac{1}{4}, \frac{5}{6}$

5. $\frac{1}{2}, \frac{1}{4}$

6. $\frac{2}{5}, \frac{3}{10}$

7. $\frac{3}{4}, \frac{1}{8}$

_____ _____ _____ _____

8. $\frac{2}{5}, \frac{1}{6}$

9. $\frac{3}{8}, \frac{1}{12}$

10. $\frac{4}{7}, \frac{3}{14}$

11. $\frac{3}{4}, \frac{2}{9}$

_____ _____ _____ _____

12. $\frac{1}{9}, \frac{2}{3}$

13. $\frac{5}{6}, \frac{3}{8}$

14. $\frac{4}{9}, \frac{2}{18}$

15. $\frac{3}{7}, \frac{2}{6}$

_____ _____ _____ _____

NUMBER SENSE

16. Name two fractions in which the LCD is the product of two denominators.

_____

Rational Numbers and the Number Line

Graph the number on the number line.

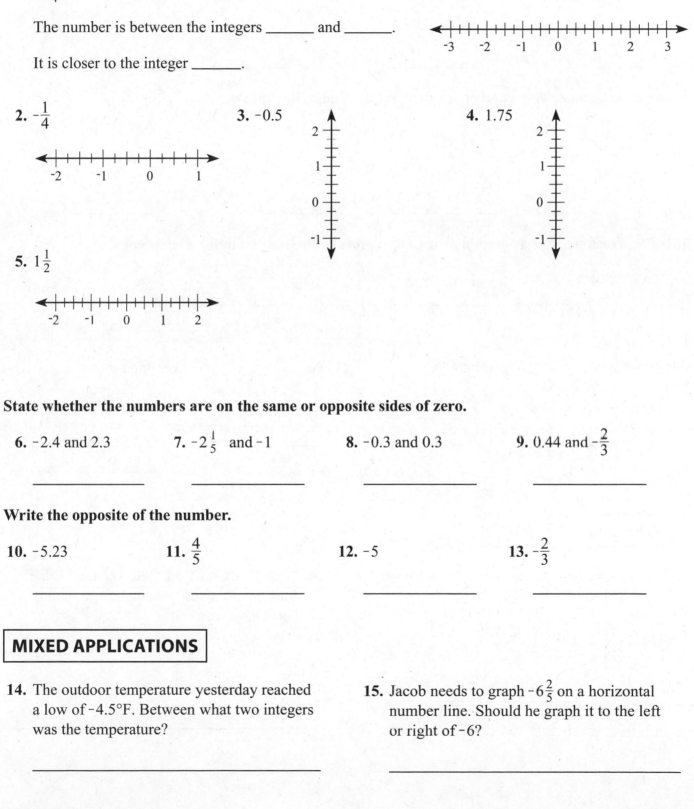

1. $-2\frac{3}{4}$

The number is between the integers _____ and _____.

It is closer to the integer _____.

2. $-\frac{1}{4}$

3. -0.5

4. 1.75

5. $1\frac{1}{2}$

State whether the numbers are on the same or opposite sides of zero.

6. -2.4 and 2.3

7. $-2\frac{1}{5}$ and -1

8. -0.3 and 0.3

9. 0.44 and $-\frac{2}{3}$

_____

_____

_____

_____

Write the opposite of the number.

10. -5.23

11. $\frac{4}{5}$

12. -5

13. $-\frac{2}{3}$

_____

_____

_____

_____

MIXED APPLICATIONS

14. The outdoor temperature yesterday reached a low of $-4.5°F$. Between what two integers was the temperature?

15. Jacob needs to graph $-6\frac{2}{5}$ on a horizontal number line. Should he graph it to the left or right of -6?

_____

_____

45

Fractions and Decimals

Write as a fraction or as a mixed number in simplest form.

1. 0.52　　　　**2.** 0.02　　　　**3.** 4.8　　　　**4.** 6.025

_____　　_____　　_____　　_____

Write as a decimal. Tell whether the decimal terminates or repeats.

5. $\frac{17}{25}$　　　　**6.** $\frac{7}{9}$　　　　**7.** $4\frac{13}{20}$　　　　**8.** $7\frac{8}{11}$

_____　　_____　　_____　　_____

Identify a decimal and a fraction or mixed number in simplest form for each point.

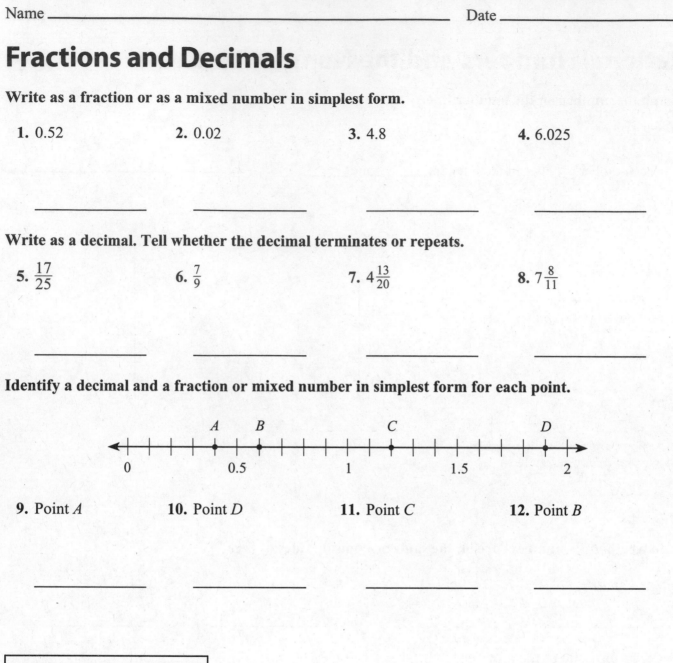

9. Point A　　　　**10.** Point D　　　　**11.** Point C　　　　**12.** Point B

_____　　_____　　_____　　_____

MIXED APPLICATIONS

13. Grace sold $\frac{5}{8}$ of her stamp collection. What is this amount as a decimal?

14. What if you scored a 0.80 on a test? What fraction of the test, in simplest form, did you answer correctly?

_____　　_____

Compare and Order Rational Numbers

Compare the numbers. Write < or >.

1. $-1\frac{1}{2}$ ◯ $-\frac{1}{2}$ Think: $-1\frac{1}{2}$ is to the _____ of $-\frac{1}{2}$ on the number line,

so $-1\frac{1}{2}$ is _____ $-\frac{1}{2}$.

2. 0.1 ◯ -1.9 **3.** 0.4 ◯ $-\frac{1}{2}$ **4.** $\frac{2}{5}$ ◯ 0.5

5. -1.1 ◯ 0 **6.** $\frac{3}{4}$ ◯ $\frac{9}{10}$ **7.** -2.5 ◯ $-\frac{3}{1}$

Order the numbers from least to greatest.

8. $0.2, -1.7, -1$ **9.** $-2\frac{3}{4}, -\frac{3}{5}, -1\frac{3}{4}$ **10.** $-0.5, -1\frac{2}{3}, -2.7$

_____ < _____ < _____   _____ < _____ < _____   _____ < _____ < _____

Order the numbers from greatest to least.

11. $-1, -\frac{5}{6}, 0$ **12.** $1.82, -\frac{2}{5}, \frac{4}{5}$ **13.** $-2.19, -2.5, 1.1$

_____ > _____ > _____   _____ > _____ > _____   _____ > _____ > _____

Write a comparison using < or > to show the relationship between the two values.

14. an elevation of -15 m and an elevation of -20.5 m

15. a balance of $78 and a balance of $-$42

16. a score of -31 points and a score of -30 points

_____   _____   _____

MIXED APPLICATIONS

17. The temperature in Cold Town on Monday was $1°C$. The temperature in Frosty Town on Monday was $-2°C$. Which town was colder on Monday?

_____

18. Stan's bank account balance is less than $-$20.00 but greater than $-$21.00. What could Stan's account balance be?

_____

Name _____   Date _____

Introduction to Algebra

Write <, >, =.

1. $25 + 3^2$ ◯ 34

2. $12.6 - 5.7$ ◯ 4.1

3. 15×6 ◯ 96

4. $132 \div 11$ ◯ 11

5. $91 - 4^2$ ◯ 25

6. $16 + 28$ ◯ 4(11)

7. $121 \div 11$ ◯ 13

8. 1.2×1.5 ◯ 1.8

9. $8^2 + 2^2$ ◯ 10^2

10. $5^2 - 4^2$ ◯ 3^2

11. 0.041 ◯ 0.41

12. 56 ◯ 55 ◯ 54

Use any of the numbers 3, 5, and 6 to write a numerical expression for each given value.

13. 27

14. 13

15. 48

_____

_____

_____

Write an example of each.

16. algebraic expression

17. algebraic equation

18. algebraic inequality

_____

_____

_____

MIXED APPLICATIONS

19. Write a numerical expression using division that shows what fraction of one dollar a penny is.

_____

20. Stan buys $5\frac{2}{3}$ yards of material at $12 per yard. What is the total cost of the material?

_____

MIXED REVIEW

Compute.

21. $15.653 - 3.92$

22. 65.01×2.1

23. $1.323 \div 2.45$

_____

_____

_____

48

Exploring Ordered Pairs

Use the map. Tell the directions needed to get from the starting point to the given location.

1. bank _____

2. police station _____

3. city hall _____

4. club house _____

5. dry cleaner _____

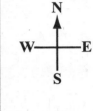

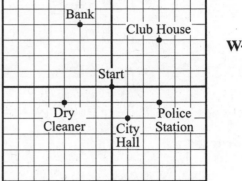

Locate each point on the map by following the given directions. Label the point with the number of the exercise.

6. Go 3 blocks east and then 4 blocks north.

7. Go 5 blocks east and then 0 blocks north.

8. Go 1 block east and then 1 block south.

9. Go 1 block west and then 2 blocks north.

10. Go 5 blocks west and then 1 block south.

11. Go 4 blocks east and then 4 blocks south.

WRITER'S CORNER

12. Write a brief story about the location of some marvel, such as buried treasure or an unknown kingdom. Giving directions like those in Exercises 6-11, tell the reader how to find this marvel, but send the searcher on many false trips as well.

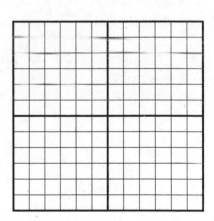

_____

_____

_____

_____

The Coordinate Plane

Write the ordered pair for each point.

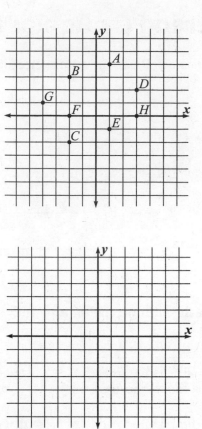

1. point A _____
2. point B _____

3. point C _____
4. point D _____

5. point E _____
6. point F _____

7. point G _____
8. point H _____

Graph each ordered pair.

9. $M(2, 3)$
10. $N(4, -5)$

11. $P(2, -2)$
12. $Q(-2, -3)$

13. $R(6, 1)$
14. $S(-4, 3)$

15. $T(3, 0)$
16. $U(0, 3)$

MIXED APPLICATIONS

Locate the points $(1, -2)$ and $(3, 2)$ on the same coordinate plane. Connect the points.

17. Find the ordered pair for another point on the line segment.

_____

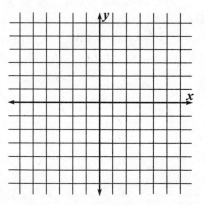

18. Suppose the points you drew are two vertices of a triangle. Find an ordered pair for the third vertex of the triangle.

_____

VISUAL THINKING

19. If you drew a horizontal line on the coordinate plane, what could you say about the y-coordinates for every point on the line?

_____

Ordered Pair Relationships

Identify the quadrant in which the point is located.

1. (10, -2) Quadrant: _____   **2.** (-5, -6) Quadrant: _____   **3.** (3, 7) Quadrant: _____

4. (-4, 9) Quadrant: _____   **5.** (8, -1) Quadrant: _____   **6.** (-11, 6) Quadrant: _____

The two points are reflections of each other across the *x*- or *y*-axis. Identify the axis.

7. (5, 3) and (-5, 3)   **8.** (-7, 1) and (-7, -1)   **9.** (-2, 4) and (-2, -4)

    axis: _____   axis: _____   axis: _____

Write the coordinates of the reflection of the point across the given axis.

10. (-6, -10), *y*-axis   **11.** (-11, 3), *x*-axis   **12.** (8, 2), *x*-axis

_____   _____   _____

MIXED APPLICATIONS

13. A town's post office is located at the point (7, 5) on a coordinate plane. In which quadrant is the post office located?

14. The grocery store is located at a point on a coordinate plane with the same *y*-coordinate as the bank but with the opposite *x*-coordinate. The grocery store and bank are reflections of each other across which axis?

_____

_____

51

Rational Numbers and the Coordinate Plane

Write the ordered pair for the point. Give approximate coordinates when necessary.

1. A

_____

2. B

_____

3. C

_____

4. D

_____

5. E

_____

6. F

_____

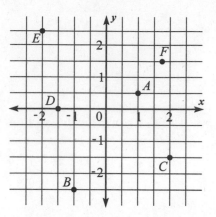

Graph and label each point on the coordinate plane.

7. $G\left(-\frac{1}{2}, 1\frac{1}{2}\right)$

8. $H(0, 2.50)$

9. $J\left(-1\frac{1}{2}, \frac{1}{2}\right)$

10. $K(1, 2)$

11. $L\left(-1\frac{1}{2}, -2\frac{1}{2}\right)$

12. $M(1, -0.5)$

13. $N\left(\frac{1}{4}, 1\frac{1}{2}\right)$

14. $P(1.25, 0)$

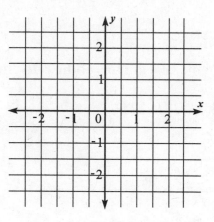

MIXED APPLICATIONS

Use the map for 15–16.

15. What is the ordered pair for the city hall?

_____

16. The post office is located at $\left(-\frac{1}{2}, 2\right)$. Graph and label a point on the map to represent the post office.

Map of Elmwood

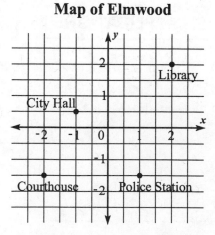

Name _____ Date _____

Distance on the Coordinate Plane

Find the distance between each pair of points. Draw a graph if necessary.

1. (1, 4) and (−3, 4)

2. (7, −2) and (11, −2)

3. (6, 4) and (6, −8)

_____ units

_____ units

_____ units

4. (8, −10) and (5, −10)

5. (−2, 26) and (−2, 5)

6. (−5, 2) and (−5, −4)

_____ units

_____ units

_____ units

Write the coordinates of a point that is the given distance from the given point.

7. 5 units from (−1, −2)

8. 8 units from (2, 4)

9. 3 units from (−7, −5)

(_____, −2)

(2, _____)

(−7, _____)

10. 6 units from (4, 21)

11. 10 units from (21, 9)

12. 7 units from (23, 2)

(4, _____)

(_____, 9)

(_____, 2)

MIXED APPLICATIONS

The map shows the locations of several areas in an amusement park. Each unit represents 10 meters.

13. How far is the Ferris wheel from the rollercoaster?

_____

14. How far is the water slide from the restrooms?

_____

Amusement Park

53

© Houghton Mifflin Harcourt Publishing Company

Unit 5
Core Skills Math, Grade 6

Figures on the Coordinate Plane

1. The vertices of triangle *DEF* are *D*(-2, 3), *E*(3, -2), and *F*(-2, -2). Graph the triangle and find the length of side $\overline{DF}$.

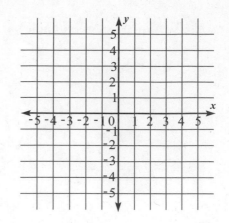

Vertical distance of *D* from 0: | 3 | = _____ units

Vertical distance of *F* from 0: | -2 | = _____ units

The points are in different quadrants, so add to find

the distance from *D* to *F*: _____ + _____ = _____ units.

Graph each figure and find the length of side $\overline{BC}$ in each figure.

2. *A*(1, 4), *B*(1, -2), *C*(-3, -2), *D*(-3, 3)

3. *A*(-1, 4), *B*(5, 4), *C*(5, 1), *D*(-1, 1)

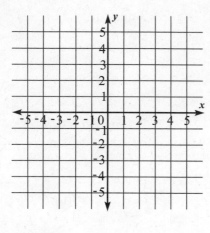

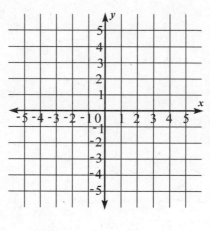

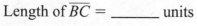

Length of $\overline{BC}$ = _____ units

Length of $\overline{BC}$ = _____ units

MIXED APPLICATIONS

4. On a map, a city block is a square with three of its vertices at (-4, 1), (1, 1), and (1, -4). What are the coordinates of the remaining vertex?

5. A carpenter is making a shelf in the shape of a parallelogram. She begins by drawing parallelogram *RSTU* on a coordinate plane with vertices *R*(1, 0), *S*(-3, 0), and *T*(-2, 3). What are the coordinates of vertex *U*?

54

Problem-Solving Strategy

WRITE A NUMBER SENTENCE

Write a number sentence to represent each problem.

1. Karen's family took 37 pictures during the first week of their camping trip. They took 45 pictures during the second week. How many pictures did they take in all?

   _____

2. Some mountain climbers have to climb 348 meters high to reach a cliff. If they can climb 1 meter in 12 minutes, how many minutes will it take them to reach the cliff?

   _____

3. The sixth-grade classes in Mindy's school went hiking. They packed their backpacks before they left. There were 63 backpacks, with 4 sandwiches in each backpack. How many sandwiches did they have?

   _____

4. In the evening 40 people went to look at the stars through telescopes. There were 8 telescopes. How many people shared each telescope?

   _____

5. About 60 hikers climbed up to the Aztec ruins. There are 5 paths to the ruins. If about the same number of hikers took each path, how many people took each path?

   _____

6. There are 28 rooms in the Kamp Hotel. If each room can hold 3 people, how many people in all can the hotel house?

   _____

MIXED APPLICATIONS

Choose a strategy and solve.

7. Christopher plans to run from 4:00 P.M. to 5:30 P.M. each day. His running pace is 12 miles per hour. How many miles will Christopher run in a week?

   _____

8. The total weight of 6 brushes is 32 grams. If each brush weighs the same amount, about how much does each brush weigh?

   _____

Using Algebraic Expressions

Use the following information to solve Exercises 1–2.

Jeff sold the pumpkins he grew for $7 each at the farmers' market.

1. Write an expression to represent the amount of money Jeff made selling the pumpkins. Tell what the variable in your expression represents.

   _____

2. If Jeff sold 30 pumpkins, how much money did he make?

   _____

Use the following information to solve Exercises 3–4.

An architect is designing a building. Each floor will be 12 feet tall.

3. Write an expression for the number of floors the building can have for a given building height. Tell what the variable in your expression represents.

   _____

4. If the architect is designing a building that is 132 feet tall, how many floors can be built?

   _____

Write an algebraic expression for each word expression. Then evaluate the expression for these values of the variable: 1, 6, and 13.5.

5. the quotient of 100 and the sum of b and 24

   _____

6. 13 more than the product of m and 5

   _____

MIXED APPLICATIONS

7. In the town of Pleasant Hill, there is an average of 16 sunny days each month. Write an expression to represent the approximate number of sunny days for any number of months. Tell what the variable represents.

   _____

8. How many sunny days can a resident of Pleasant Hill expect to have in 9 months?

   _____

Problem-Solving Strategy

WRITE AN EQUATION

Write and solve an equation for each exercise.

1. Vicki is saving money to buy some sports equipment that costs $116. She already has saved $68. How much more does she need to save?

   _____

2. Steve was 46 years old 9 years ago. How old is Steve now?

   _____

3. A recipe for fruit salad calls for $1\frac{1}{2}$ cups of nuts. Sam has $2\frac{1}{4}$ cups of nuts. How many cups of nuts will Sam have left after he makes the fruit salad?

   _____

4. The cost of a TV after a discount of $550 is $1,360. What was the original cost of the TV?

   _____

MIXED APPLICATIONS

Choose a strategy and solve.

5. Connie is 4 years older than Carla. The sum of their ages is 28. How old is Carla?

   _____

6. An equilateral triangle has a perimeter of 27 m. What is the length of each side of the triangle?

   _____

WRITER'S CORNER

7. Write a problem that can be solved with this equation: $x - 5 = 15$.

   _____

   _____

   _____

Problem Solving

FRACTION OPERATIONS

Read each problem and solve.

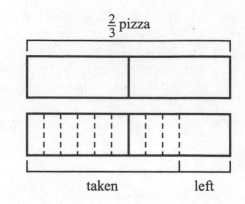

$\frac{2}{3}$ pizza

taken   left

1. $\frac{2}{3}$ of a pizza was left over. A group of friends divided the leftover pizza into pieces each equal to $\frac{1}{18}$ of the original pizza. After each friend took one piece, $\frac{1}{4}$ of the leftover pizza remained. How many friends were in the group? The figures represent the pizza.

   _____

2. Sarah's craft project uses pieces of yarn that are $\frac{1}{8}$ yard long. She has a piece of yarn that is 3 yards long. How many $\frac{1}{8}$-yard pieces can she cut and still have $1\frac{1}{4}$ yards left?

   _____

3. Alex opens a 1-pint container of orange butter. He spreads $\frac{1}{16}$ of the butter on his bread. Then he divides the rest of the butter into $\frac{3}{4}$-pint containers. How many $\frac{3}{4}$-pint containers is he able to fill?

   _____

4. Kaitlin buys $\frac{9}{10}$ pound of candy orange slices. She eats $\frac{1}{3}$ of them and divides the rest equally into 3 bags. How much is in each bag?

   _____

Problem Solving

APPLY THE GREATEST COMMON FACTOR

Solve each problem.

1. Ashley is bagging 32 pumpkin muffins and 28 banana muffins for some friends. Each bag will hold only one type of muffin. Each bag will hold the same number of muffins. What is the greatest number of muffins she can put in each bag? How many bags of each type of muffin will there be?

_____

2. Patricia is separating 16 soccer cards and 22 baseball cards into groups. Each group will have the same number of cards, and each group will have only one kind of sports card. What is the greatest number of cards she can put in each group? How many groups of each type will there be?

_____

3. Bryan is setting chairs in rows for a graduation ceremony. He has 50 black chairs and 60 white chairs. Each row will have the same number of chairs, and each row will have the same color chair. What is the greatest number of chairs that he can fit in each row? How many rows of each color chair will there be?

_____

4. A store clerk is bagging spices. He has 18 teaspoons of cinnamon and 30 teaspoons of nutmeg. Each bag needs to contain the same number of teaspoons, and each bag can contain only one spice. How many teaspoons of spice should the clerk put in each bag? How many bags of each spice will there be?

_____

5. A teacher is placing counters in bags for students. There are 24 blue counters and 56 yellow counters. Each bag needs to have the same number of counters, and each bag can contain only one color. How many counters should the teacher place in each bag, and how many bags of each color will there be?

_____

Problem Solving

THE COORDINATE PLANE

Solve each problem.

1. On a coordinate map of Clifton, an electronics store is located at (6, -7). A convenience store is located 7 units north of the electronics store on the map. What are the map coordinates of the convenience store?

    _____

2. Sonya and Lucas walk from the school to the library. They walk 5 blocks south and 4 blocks west to get to the library. If the school is located at a point (9, -1) on a coordinate map, what are the map coordinates of the library?

    _____

3. On a coordinate map, Sherry's house is at the point (10, -2) and the mall is at point (-4, -2). If each unit on the map represents one block, what is the distance between Sherry's house and the mall?

    _____

4. Arthur left his job at (5, 4) on a coordinate map and walked to his house at (5, -6). Each unit on the map represents 1 block. How far did Arthur walk?

    _____

5. A fire station is located 2 units east and 6 units north of a hospital. If the hospital is located at a point (-2, -3) on a coordinate map, what are the coordinates of the fire station?

    _____

6. Xavier's house is located at the point (4, 6). Michael's house is 10 blocks west and 2 blocks south of Xavier's house. What are the coordinates of Michael's house?

    _____

7. On a coordinate map, a pizzeria is located at (9, 3). A pizza is being delivered to a house located at (9, -3). Each unit represents 1 mile. How far is the pizzeria from the house?

    _____

Exploring Percent

The table shows the results of a survey that asked families which restaurant they liked the best. Use the table for Exercises 1–5.

Favorite Restaurant	
Restaurant	**Number of Votes***
Miguel's	30
Mario's	35
Monday's	15
Maxie's	20
*from a total of 100 surveyed	

1. What percent of those surveyed prefer Mario's?

   _____

2. What percent of those surveyed do not prefer Monday's?

   _____

3. Is any one restaurant preferred by more than half of the people surveyed?

   _____

4. Suppose that the numbers of votes remained the same except that 30 people preferred Maxie's. Would that mean that 30% of those surveyed preferred Maxie's? Explain.

   _____

   _____

Tell what percent of one dollar is shown.

5.

   _____

6.

   _____

7.

   _____

Solve.

8. If you surveyed 50 people and 40 said *yes* to a question, what percent of the people said yes? Explain.

   _____

9. Prices at a store are reduced by 20%. How much do you save on 6 items that cost $1.00 each?

   _____

EVERYDAY MATH CONNECTION

10. List three vitamins in your favorite cereal. Compare the percentage of U.S. recommended daily allowance of each vitamin for the cereal alone and for the cereal with milk. What do you discover?

   _____

Exploring Dividing Fractions

Complete.

1. How many fives are in twenty-five? _____

2. How many fours are in twelve? _____

3. How many threes are in twelve? _____

Write a division number sentence for each picture.

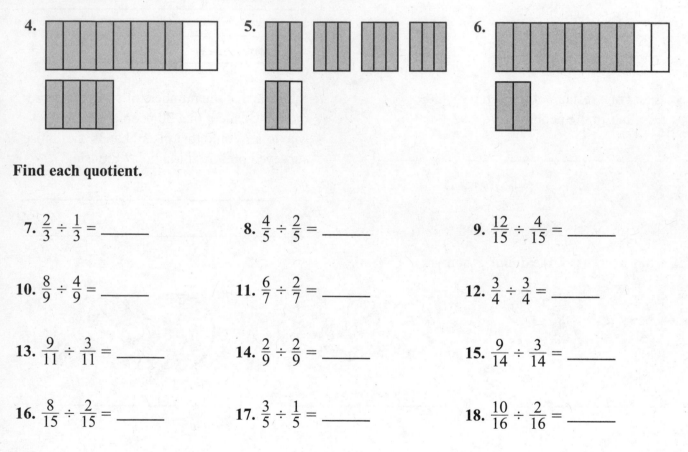

4.

5.

6.

Find each quotient.

7. $\dfrac{2}{3} \div \dfrac{1}{3} =$ _____

8. $\dfrac{4}{5} \div \dfrac{2}{5} =$ _____

9. $\dfrac{12}{15} \div \dfrac{4}{15} =$ _____

10. $\dfrac{8}{9} \div \dfrac{4}{9} =$ _____

11. $\dfrac{6}{7} \div \dfrac{2}{7} =$ _____

12. $\dfrac{3}{4} \div \dfrac{3}{4} =$ _____

13. $\dfrac{9}{11} \div \dfrac{3}{11} =$ _____

14. $\dfrac{2}{9} \div \dfrac{2}{9} =$ _____

15. $\dfrac{9}{14} \div \dfrac{3}{14} =$ _____

16. $\dfrac{8}{15} \div \dfrac{2}{15} =$ _____

17. $\dfrac{3}{5} \div \dfrac{1}{5} =$ _____

18. $\dfrac{10}{16} \div \dfrac{2}{16} =$ _____

SCIENCE CONNECTION

19. Our solar system consists of eight major planets, including
Earth. Jupiter, the largest planet, has an equatorial diameter
of 88,000 miles. Uranus has an equatorial diameter $\dfrac{4}{11}$ the
size of Jupiter's. What is the equatorial diameter of Uranus?

Exploring Division of Fractions

Look for a pattern in the division and multiplication number sentences.

1. $8 \div 2 =$ _____ $8 \times \frac{1}{2} =$ _____   2. $2 \div \frac{1}{2} =$ _____ $2 \times \frac{2}{1} =$ _____

3. $4 \div \frac{4}{3} =$ _____ $4 \times \frac{3}{4} =$ _____   4. $\frac{1}{5} \div \frac{1}{2} =$ _____ $\frac{1}{5} \times \frac{2}{1} =$ _____

5. For each pair of number sentences, what is the product
   of the divisor in the division sentence and the second
   factor in the multiplication sentence?

   _____

Write the reciprocal of each divisor.

6. $8 \div \frac{1}{3}$ ___   7. $6 \div \frac{2}{5}$ ___   8. $\frac{2}{3} \div 4$ ___   9. $\frac{4}{5} \div 5$ ___   10. $\frac{3}{4} \div \frac{2}{3}$ ___

11. $4 \div \frac{1}{7}$ ___   12. $5 \div \frac{2}{9}$ ___   13. $\frac{2}{5} \div \frac{3}{8}$ ___   14. $\frac{7}{8} \div \frac{1}{8}$ ___   15. $\frac{6}{11} \div \frac{5}{7}$ ___

16. $\frac{4}{7} \div \frac{3}{5}$ ___   17. $\frac{9}{10} \div \frac{1}{16}$ ___   18. $\frac{2}{3} \div \frac{2}{3}$ ___   19. $\frac{1}{5} \div \frac{4}{5}$ ___   20. $20 \div \frac{1}{20}$ ___

Complete the multiplication sentence to find the quotient of each division sentence.

21. $\frac{2}{3} \div \frac{1}{5} =$ ___ $\frac{2}{3} \times$ ___ $=$ ___   22. $\frac{2}{3} \div \frac{1}{6} =$ ___ $\frac{2}{3} \times$ ___ $=$ ___

23. $\frac{5}{8} \div \frac{3}{4} =$ ___ $\frac{5}{8} \times$ ___ $=$ ___   24. $\frac{1}{7} : \frac{2}{3} =$ ___ $\frac{1}{7} \times$ ___ $=$ ___

25. $\frac{4}{5} \div \frac{3}{7} =$ ___ $\frac{4}{5} \times$ ___ $=$ ___   26. $\frac{5}{6} \div \frac{1}{4} =$ ___ $\frac{5}{6} \times$ ___ $=$ ___

27. $\frac{3}{8} \div \frac{8}{9} =$ ___ $\frac{3}{8} \times$ ___ $=$ ___   28. $\frac{4}{9} \div \frac{2}{7} =$ ___ $\frac{4}{9} \times$ ___ $=$ ___

29. $\frac{4}{7} \div \frac{1}{4} =$ ___ $\frac{4}{7} \times$ ___ $=$ ___   30. $\frac{7}{8} \div \frac{2}{5} =$ ___ $\frac{7}{8} \times$ ___ $=$ ___

31. $\frac{3}{10} \div \frac{1}{5} =$ ___ $\frac{3}{10} \times$ ___ $=$ ___   32. $\frac{2}{3} \div \frac{2}{5} =$ ___ $\frac{2}{3} \times$ ___ $=$ ___

LOGICAL REASONING

33. When you divide a number by $\frac{1}{2}$, the quotient is 6 more
    than the product of the number and $\frac{1}{2}$. What is the number?

Name _____ Date _____

Dividing Fractions

Complete.

1. $\frac{1}{3} \div \frac{1}{2} = \frac{1}{3} \times \frac{2}{1} =$ _____

2. $8 \div \frac{1}{4} = 8 \times$ ____ = ____

3. $4 \div \frac{4}{5} =$ ____ $\times \frac{5}{4} =$ ____

4. $\frac{1}{3} \div \frac{3}{5} = \frac{1}{3} \times$ ____ = ____

Tell whether each quotient will be greater than or less than 1.

5. $10 \div \frac{1}{3}$ _____

6. $12 \div \frac{3}{4}$ _____

7. $\frac{3}{8} \div \frac{2}{3}$ _____

8. $\frac{3}{5} \div \frac{1}{4}$ _____

9. $\frac{7}{8} \div \frac{2}{9}$ _____

10. $\frac{9}{10} \div \frac{3}{5}$ _____

11. $1 \div \frac{5}{2}$ _____

12. $8 \div \frac{2}{3}$ _____

Find each quotient.

13. $10 \div \frac{4}{5} =$ _____

14. $5 \div \frac{2}{5} =$ _____

15. $\frac{2}{3} \div \frac{4}{7} =$ _____

16. $\frac{7}{8} \div \frac{1}{2} =$ _____

17. $9 \div \frac{3}{7} =$ _____

18. $12 \div \frac{3}{4} =$ _____

19. $\frac{3}{4} \div \frac{1}{12} =$ _____

20. $\frac{4}{7} \div \frac{3}{14} =$ _____

21. $6 \div \frac{3}{5} =$ _____

22. $\frac{9}{10} \div \frac{3}{7} =$ _____

23. $4 \div \frac{5}{6} =$ _____

24. $\frac{2}{5} \div \frac{3}{10} =$ _____

25. $\frac{2}{3} \div \frac{2}{5} =$ _____

26. $\frac{2}{5} \div \frac{1}{6} =$ _____

27. $\frac{5}{6} \div \frac{1}{2} =$ _____

28. $\frac{11}{9} \div \frac{8}{3} =$ _____

29. $\frac{1}{2} \div \frac{5}{8} =$ _____

30. $\frac{8}{9} \div \frac{1}{9} =$ _____

31. $\frac{4}{5} \div \frac{2}{5} =$ _____

32. $\frac{3}{5} \div \frac{3}{4} =$ _____

MIXED APPLICATIONS

33. Alex has $\frac{5}{6}$ can of popcorn. If it takes $\frac{1}{8}$ can to make 1 serving, how many servings can he make?

_____

34. It takes $\frac{2}{3}$ second to clap your hands. How many times can you clap in 60 seconds?

_____

NUMBER SENSE

35. The sum of a number and its reciprocal is $5\frac{1}{5}$. What is the number?

_____

Model Mixed Number Division

Use the model to find the quotient.

1. $4\frac{1}{2} \div \frac{1}{2} =$ _____

2. $3\frac{1}{3} \div \frac{1}{6} =$ _____

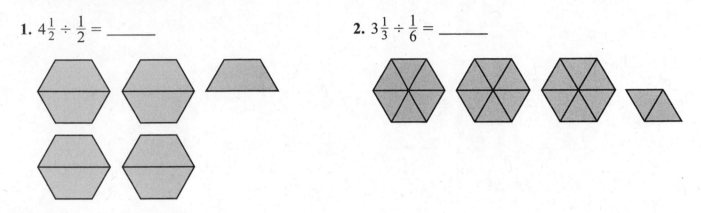

Find each quotient. Then draw the model.

3. $2\frac{1}{2} \div \frac{1}{6} =$ _____

4. $1\frac{1}{2} \div \frac{1}{2} =$ _____

5. $2\frac{3}{4} \div 2 =$ _____

6. $3\frac{1}{3} \div 3 =$ _____

MIXED APPLICATIONS

7. Marty has $2\frac{4}{5}$ quarts of juice. He pours the same amount of juice into 2 bottles. How much does he pour into each bottle?

_____

8. How many $\frac{1}{3}$-pound servings are in $4\frac{2}{3}$ pounds of cheese?

_____

Dividing Mixed Numbers

Write each as a multiplication sentence.

1. $2\frac{1}{4} \div \frac{1}{8}$ _____

2. $\frac{5}{6} \div 1\frac{1}{2}$ _____

3. $2\frac{1}{3} \div 4$ _____

4. $1\frac{1}{5} \div 5\frac{2}{3}$ _____

Find each quotient.

5. $1\frac{1}{4} \div \frac{2}{5} =$ _____

6. $3\frac{3}{5} \div \frac{2}{3} =$ _____

7. $\frac{3}{8} \div 1\frac{1}{2} =$ _____

8. $2\frac{1}{5} \div 1\frac{3}{4} =$ _____

9. $2\frac{2}{3} \div 6\frac{1}{2} =$ _____

10. $4 \div 1\frac{4}{7} =$ _____

11. $3\frac{1}{2} \div 1\frac{3}{5} =$ _____

12. $6\frac{2}{3} \div 2\frac{1}{2} =$ _____

13. $1\frac{1}{5} \div \frac{2}{15} =$ _____

14. $3\frac{3}{7} \div 1\frac{1}{3} =$ _____

15. $8 \div 4\frac{4}{5} =$ _____

16. $6\frac{2}{3} \div 1\frac{1}{9} =$ _____

17. $5 \div 3\frac{1}{3} =$ _____

18. $6\frac{1}{2} \div 2\frac{1}{6} =$ _____

19. $8 \div 6\frac{1}{2} =$ _____

20. $6\frac{1}{2} \div 1\frac{1}{2} =$ _____

21. $2\frac{1}{4} \div \frac{1}{8} =$ _____

22. $\frac{5}{6} \div 1\frac{1}{2} =$ _____

23. $2\frac{1}{3} \div 4 =$ _____

24. $1\frac{1}{5} \div 3\frac{1}{3} =$ _____

MIXED APPLICATIONS

25. A piece of material 10 feet long will be cut into pieces to use in a craft project. Each piece of material will be $1\frac{1}{4}$ ft long. How many pieces of material can be cut?

_____

26. It took Bart $\frac{3}{4}$ hour to write one story. He wrote 8 stories. How long did he spend writing stories?

_____

MIXED REVIEW

Tell whether each product will be greater than or less than 1.

27. $\frac{2}{3} \times \frac{1}{2}$ _____

28. $\frac{1}{4} \times 84$ _____

29. $36 \times \frac{1}{7}$ _____

30. $\frac{8}{9} \times \frac{3}{4}$ _____

Find each product.

31. $0.45 \times 0.9 =$ _____

32. $23 \times 2.05 =$ _____

33. $9.06 \times 5.7 =$ _____

34. $13.8 \times 4.4 =$ _____

35. $\frac{4}{5} \times \frac{3}{4} =$ _____

36. $12 \times 1\frac{2}{5} =$ _____

37. $2\frac{1}{4} \times 1\frac{1}{2} =$ _____

38. $4\frac{2}{3} \times 1\frac{2}{9} =$ _____

Find each quotient.

39. $\frac{1}{4} \div \frac{1}{5} =$ _____

40. $6 \div \frac{12}{13} =$ _____

41. $\frac{1}{9} \div \frac{2}{3} =$ _____

42. $8 \div \frac{5}{12} =$ _____

Relating Metric Units

Complete each pattern.

1. 0.002 L = 2 mL

 0.02 L = _____ mL

 0.2 L = _____ mL

 2 L = _____ mL

2. 0.001 m = 1 mm

 0.01 m = _____ mm

 0.1 m = _____ mm

 1 m = _____ mm

3. 2 kg = 2,000 g

 0.2 kg = _____ g

 0.02 kg = _____ g

 0.002 kg = _____ g

Find each missing number.

4. 5 m = _____ km

5. 6 mL = _____ L

6. 3 mm = _____ m

7. 125 g = _____ kg

8. 0.25 m = _____ km

9. 360 cm = _____ m

10. 0.97 kL = _____ L

11. 3,000 g = _____ kg

12. 340 mm = _____ cm

13. 9 L = _____ mL

14. 2.1 m = _____ mm

15. 1 m = _____ km

16. 0.076 L = _____ mL

17. 35 cm = _____ mm

18. 14 km = _____ m

19. 3.9 kL = _____ L

20. 400 mm = _____ cm

21. 6.3 L = _____ mL

MIXED APPLICATIONS

22. If Mrs. Stevens fills her watering can with 1,750 mL of water, how many liters is she using?

_____

23. Joey weighs 62 kg. Tony weighs 68 kg. How many grams do they weigh together?

_____

NUMBER SENSE

24. Kaye has two 750 mL cans of juice. She wants to put the juice in a 1.5 L pitcher. Will the pitcher hold all of the juice? Explain your answer.

_____

_____

Metric Units of Capacity and Mass

Change to the given unit.

1. 3 mL = _____ L

2. 0.24 L = _____ mL

3. 1,350 mL = _____ L

4. 20 kg = _____ g

5. 0.4 g = _____ kg

6. 310 g = _____ kg

7. 35 L = _____ mL

8. 5.7 L = _____ ml

9. 20,000 mL = _____ L

10. 33,000 g = _____ kg

11. 3.6 kg = _____ g

12. 560 g = _____ kg

13. 45,000 mL = _____ L

14. 6.5 g = _____ kg

15. 780 g = _____ kg

16. 35,050 mL = _____ L

17. 6.8 L = _____ mL

18. 26 g = _____ kg

19. 230 mL = _____ L

20. 47 g = _____ kg

21. 0.24 kg = _____ g

22. 177 kg = _____ g

23. 456 L = _____ mL

24. 1.76 L = _____ mL

MIXED APPLICATIONS

25. Taro has marbles whose total mass is 24 g. If each marble has a mass of about 1.5 g, how may marbles does Taro have?

_____

26. The mass of a large egg is about 60 g. What is the mass in kilograms of a dozen large eggs?

_____

27. A water tank has a mass of 3.6 kg when it is empty. The same tank has a mass of 51.5 kg when it is full of water. What is the mass of the water when the tank is full?

_____

28. The capacity of a small glass is 120 mL. How many small glasses can be filled from a 500-mL pitcher of milk?

_____

NUMBER SENSE

29. A serving of soup is 400 mL. Maria made 2.5 L of soup. Is that enough soup to serve 5 people? Explain your answer.

_____

Customary Units of Length

Estimate each product or quotient.

1. 35 ft × 12 = _____ in.

2. 3,063 ft ÷ 3 = _____ yd

3. 614 yd × 3 = _____ ft

4. 35,567 ft ÷ 5,280 = _____ mi

5. 75,233 in. ÷ 36 = _____ yd

6. 5,280 × 43 mi = _____ ft

Tell what number to multiply or divide by to change units. Then change the units.

7. 36 feet to inches

8. 21,120 feet to miles

9. 66 feet to yards

_____

_____

_____

Change to the given units.

10. 346 ft = _____ yd _____ ft

11. 8,000 ft = _____ mi _____ ft

12. 245 ft = _____ yd _____ ft

13. 4 mi = _____ yd

Change to the given unit. Write the remainder in fraction form.

14. 24 in. = _____ yd

15. 1,760 ft = _____ mi

16. 86 in. = _____ ft

MIXED APPLICATIONS

17. If each table is 96 in. long, how many yards of paper will it take to cover 4 tables?

    _____

18. Bert is $6\frac{1}{2}$ ft tall. How many inches tall is he?

    _____

NUMBER SENSE

19. The entrance to a golf course is lined with 8-inch long bricks. One row of the bricks is one mile long. Are 5,280 bricks enough for one row? Explain your reasoning.

_____

_____

Customary Units of Capacity and Weight

Change to the given unit.

1. 3 c = _____ fl oz

2. 2 qt = _____ pt

3. 48 oz = _____ lb

4. 8 lb = _____ oz

5. 8 lb 3 oz = _____ oz

6. $\frac{1}{2}$ T = _____ lb

7. $2\frac{1}{2}$ gal = _____ qt

8. $1\frac{3}{4}$ lb = _____ oz

9. 16 qt = _____ gal

10. 36 pt = _____ qt

11. 12 oz = _____ lb

12. 4,000 lb = _____ T

13. 24 oz = _____ lb

14. 136 fl oz = _____ pt

15. $12\frac{1}{2}$ c = _____ fl oz

16. $12\frac{1}{2}$ pt = _____ c

17. $16\frac{1}{4}$ lb = _____ oz

18. $2\frac{1}{2}$ T = _____ lb

MIXED APPLICATIONS

19. Carol has a 1-qt carton of orange juice. Does she have enough juice to fill eight 4-oz glasses?

_____

20. Lynd's Fruit Farm sold 1,250 baskets of apples this year. Each basket weighed an average of 18 pounds. How many tons of apples were sold?

_____

21. Cora used 3 gallons of milk one week. The next week she used 16 quarts. During which week did she use more?

_____

22. Doba weighs 95 pounds. His father weighs 165 pounds. How much more does his father weigh?

_____

EVERYDAY MATH CONNECTION

Missy works at a clothing factory. Last week she made 8 skirts and 12 blouses. She used 5 ft of fabric to make each skirt and 4 ft of fabric to make each blouse.

23. Was more fabric used to make skirts or blouses?

_____

24. Did she use more than 25 yards of fabric? Explain.

_____

Exploring Solid Figures

Name each solid. Then write the number of vertices (*V*), edges (*E*), and faces (*F*).

1.

V _____

E _____

F _____

_____

2.

V _____

E _____

F _____

_____

3.

V _____

E _____

F _____

_____

4.

V _____

E _____

F _____

_____

Name the shapes needed and the number of each you would use to build the solid.

5. cylinder

_____

6. square pyramid

_____

7. rectangular prism

_____

Solve.

8. Shawn has four congruent triangles. What solid figure can he make?

_____

9. Add the number of faces and vertices in each figure in Exercises 1-4. Compare this sum to the number of edges. What do you notice?

_____

_____

10. Janna has four congruent triangles and a square. What solid figure can she make?

_____

_____

LOGICAL REASONING

11. Kasa, Lola, and Leroy live in Kentucky, Iowa, and Louisiana. No one lives in a state that begins with the same letter as the person's name. Lola and the person from Iowa went to the same university. Where does each person live?

_____

© Houghton Mifflin Harcourt Publishing Company

Name _____   Date _____

Solid Figures

Complete the table by naming the type of solid figure.

	Type of Solid Figure	Number of Bases and Faces	Number of Edges	Number of Vertices
1.		1 base 4 other faces	8	5
2.		2 bases 8 other faces	24	16
3.		1 base	none	none
4.		2 bases 3 other faces	9	6
5.		1 base 5 other faces	10	6

MIXED APPLICATIONS

6. Name three objects in your classroom that are examples of solid figures.

_____

_____

7. Name three useful common objects that are shaped like rectangular prisms. Why do you think each object is shaped like this?

_____

_____

MIXED REVIEW

Complete.

8. 8.65 kg = _____ g

9. 220 mL = _____ L

10. 2 yd = _____ in.

11. 48 oz = _____ lb

12. 10 lb = _____ oz

13. 5 qt = _____ pt

14. 3 c = _____ oz

Three-Dimensional Figures

Name each figure.

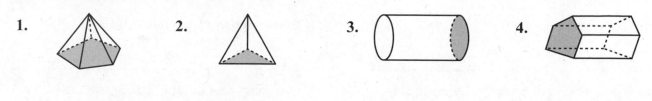

1. _____ 2. _____ 3. _____ 4. _____

The faces, or surfaces, of some three-dimensional figures are shown. Name the figure. Is each a polyhedron? Write *yes* or *no*.

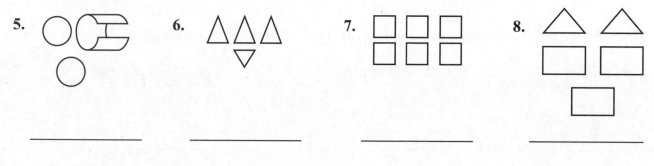

5. _____ 6. _____ 7. _____ 8. _____

_____ _____ _____ _____

Complete the table.

Polyhedron	Number of Faces	Number of Vertices	Number of Edges
9. pentagonal prism			
10. pentagonal pyramid			
11. octagonal prism			
12. octagonal pyramid			

VISUAL THINKING

Imagine a cube formed by folding the pattern shown.

13. Which faces would be opposite each other?
    Write the pairs of numbers of these faces.

_____

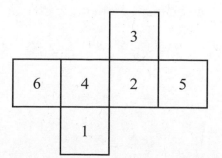

Name _____ Date _____

Solid Figures (Polyhedra)

Write *pyramid* or *prism* to describe each polyhedron. Then write the specific name for each.

1. one rectangular base; other faces, triangles

_____ ; _____

2. four congruent triangles

_____ ; _____

3. one pentagonal base; other faces, triangles

_____ ; _____

4. two congruent parallel hexagonal bases; other faces, parallelograms

_____ ; _____

Describe each polyhedron. Include the shape of the base, or bases, and the shape of the other faces.

5. square prism

_____

_____

6. triangular prism

_____

_____

7. rectangular prism

_____

_____

MIXED APPLICATIONS

8. Mike's fish tank is a prism with a pentagonal base, each side measuring 8 inches. What is the base perimeter of his fish tank?

_____

_____

9. Alice wants to build a box for her TV. Which design is better: a rectangular prism or a rectangular pyramid? Explain your answer.

_____

_____

VISUAL THINKING

10. Write the letter of the polyhedron that can be made from this pattern.

_____

a. pentagonal prism

b. square prism

c. octagonal pyramid

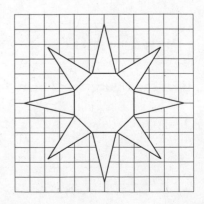

Name _____ Date _____

Exploring Ratio

Write each ratio in three ways.

1. triangles to rectangles

_____

2. rectangles to all shapes

_____

3. stars to circles

_____

4. circles to stars

_____

5. all shapes to stars

_____

6. circles to rectangles

_____

Write *part to whole*, *whole to part*, or *part to part* for each description in Exercises 1–6.

7. Exercise 1

_____

8. Exercise 2

_____

9. Exercise 3

_____

10. Exercise 4

_____

11. Exercise 5

_____

12. Exercise 6

_____

13. There are 10 girls and 8 boys in a class. What is the ratio of boys to girls?

_____

14. There are 20 men and 10 women on a bus. What is the ratio of men to the total number of people?

_____

SOCIAL STUDIES CONNECTION

15. The state of Texas is about 6 times the size of the state of New Jersey. The state of Pennsylvania is half the size of the state of Texas. What is the ratio of the size of New Jersey to the size of Pennsylvania?

_____

Ratios

Draw a picture to show each ratio.

1. The ratio of green circles to purple circles is 3:4.

2. The ratio of red hats to blue hats is two to three.

_____

3. The ratio of trees to flowers is $\frac{5}{2}$.

4. The ratio of dogs to cats is 1:4.

_____

Write each ratio in two other ways.

5. twelve to five _____

6. 6:7 _____

7. fifteen to twenty-one _____

8. $\frac{8}{3}$ _____

9. 40:3 _____

10. $\frac{7}{18}$ _____

MIXED APPLICATIONS

11. Mr. Tull bought 6 paperback books and 5 hardcover books. What is the ratio of paperback books to the total number of books?

12. There are 8 fish in 3 ponds. What is the ratio of fish to ponds?

NUMBER SENSE

13. Candi invited 83 students to a cookout. If she invited 29 girls, what is the ratio of girls to boys invited?

_____

Rates

Write a ratio that describes each rate.

1. 3 jars for $1.99 _____

2. a dozen bagels for $2.99 _____

3. 26 mi per gal _____

4. 45 revolutions per min _____

5. 4 lb for $2.50 _____

6. 7 for one dollar _____

7. 55 mi per hour _____

8. 12 for $2 _____

Find each unit rate or unit price.

9. 6 for $1.20 _____

10. $1.56 a dozen _____

11. 279 mi per 9 gal _____

12. 5 lb for $2.50 _____

13. 2 hours for $76 _____

14. 16 for $58.40 _____

15. $40 for 8 _____

16. $135 for 6 hours of work _____

MIXED APPLICATIONS

17. An office supply store sells report covers at 3 for $0.96. If the rate remains the same, how much will 10 covers cost?

_____

18. Marilee buys 8 bottles of apple juice for $10. What is the unit price of each bottle?

_____

19. This summer Andrea's family will rent a cabin in the mountains for two weeks. The total cost is $500. About how much does the cabin cost per day?

_____

20. Andrea's car gets 25 miles per gallon of gas. Her vacation cabin is 190 miles away. How many gallons of gas will she need to get there?

_____

NUMBER SENSE

20. Ben drove 350 miles in $6\frac{1}{2}$ hours. Marcie drove 520 miles in $12\frac{1}{4}$ hours. Who drove faster?

_____

Unit Rates

Write a ratio in fraction form for each rate. Use equivalent fractions to solve.

1. 15 yd for 5 dresses
   ☐ yd for 2 dresses

   _____

2. 42 days in 6 wk
   14 days in ☐ wk

   _____

3. 16 eggs for 4 omelets
   ☐ eggs for 2 omelets

   _____

4. 6 mi in 30 min
   8 mi in ☐ min

   _____

5. $50 for 2 classes
   $☐ for 3 classes

   _____

6. 150 km in 2 hr
   ☐ km in 1 hr

   _____

Write each unit rate in fraction form.

7. 690 mi in 3 days

   _____

8. $300 in 20 days

   _____

9. 600 flowers/30 bouquets

   _____

10. 360 beads/12 necklaces

    _____

11. $54 in 9 hr

    _____

12. 336 mi/12 gal

    _____

13. 258 km/3 hr

    _____

14. $2.66/7 L

    _____

15. 232 mi in 16 hr

    _____

MIXED APPLICATIONS

16. Tera can jog 5.5 mi in one hour. At the same rate, how far can she jog in 2 hours?

    _____

17. Joe can jog 6 mi in one hour. How much farther than Tera can he jog in 2 hours?

    _____

WRITER'S CORNER

18. Write a word problem to fit the following rates: 72 tokens/12 games, ■ tokens/10 games.

    _____

    _____

Writing Ratios

Write two ratios that are equivalent to the given ratio.

1. 3:5 _____

2. 4:5 _____

3. 1:7 _____

4. 6:9 _____

5. $\frac{2}{10}$ _____

6. $\frac{6}{18}$ _____

Tell whether the ratios are equivalent. Write _yes_ or _no_.

7. $\frac{3}{7}$ and $\frac{3}{8}$ _____

8. 2:6 and 4:12 _____

9. 6 to 8 and 8 to 10 _____

10. $\frac{2}{7}$ and $\frac{4}{14}$ _____

11. 1:10 and 2:20 _____

12. $\frac{4}{5}$ and $\frac{2}{10}$ _____

13. Use multiplication to write two ratios that are equivalent to $\frac{3}{8}$.

_____

14. Use division to write two ratios that are equivalent to $\frac{12}{18}$.

_____

MIXED APPLICATIONS

15. There are 4 boys and 12 girls in Class A. There are 8 boys and 24 girls in Class B. What are the ratios of boys to girls in each class? Are the ratios the same?

_____

16. One week, John ate 2 bananas and 5 apples. The next week, he ate two times the number of apples and bananas. How many apples and bananas did he eat?

_____

EVERYDAY MATH CONNECTION

17. A truck driver earns $10 per hour, and an engineer earns $20 per hour. If the truck driver made $360 this week, how many hours did he work? How many hours would it take the engineer to make the same amount of money?

_____

Equivalent Ratios

Write two ratios that are equivalent to the given ratio.

1. $\frac{2}{3}$

_____

2. 4:5

_____

3. 5 to 6

_____

4. 8:5

_____

5. 3 to 1

_____

6. $\frac{6}{7}$

_____

7. $\frac{9}{2}$

_____

8. 4 to 9

_____

Tell whether the ratios are equivalent. Write *yes* or *no*.

9. $\frac{3}{4}$; $\frac{6}{8}$ _____

10. 5:6; 10:15 _____

11. 1:4; 5:20 _____

12. $\frac{3}{7}$; $\frac{10}{21}$ _____

13. $\frac{24}{36}$; $\frac{2}{3}$ _____

14. 45:50; 5:10 _____

15. $\frac{12}{18}$; $\frac{6}{9}$ _____

16. 16:40; 8:20 _____

Find the term that makes the ratios equivalent.

17. $\frac{2}{3}$; $\frac{\Box}{15}$

18. $\frac{\Box}{4}$; $\frac{3}{12}$

19. 5 to 6; 10 to $\Box$

20. 10 to 2; $\Box$ to 8

21. $\frac{15}{3}$; $\frac{5}{\Box}$

22. $\frac{\Box}{8}$; $\frac{3}{1}$

23. 6 to 3; 12 to $\Box$

24. 24:10; 12: $\Box$

MIXED APPLICATIONS

25. Gerry is a member of a book club. He gets 2 books free for every 7 books he buys. If he bought 21 books last year, how many books did he get free?

_____

26. Juan rented 24 movies at $2.75 each. What was the total cost for renting the movies?

_____

NUMBER SENSE

27. Joe wrote a play. It takes the actors 5 minutes to act out 2 pages of the script. If Joe's script is 106 pages long, how long is the play?

_____

Finding Unit Rates

Write each rate as a fraction. Then find each unit rate.

1. A wheel rotates through 1,800°
   in 5 revolutions.

   _____

2. There are 312 cards in 6 decks
   of playing cards.

   _____

3. Bana ran 18.6 miles of a marathon in 3 hours.

   _____

4. Cameron paid $30.16 for 8 pounds
   of almonds.

   _____

Compare unit rates.

5. An online game company offers a package
   that includes 2 games for $11.98. They also
   offer a package that includes 5 games for
   $24.95. Which package is a better deal?

   _____

6. At a track meet, Samma finished the
   200-meter race in 25.98 seconds. Tom
   finished the 100-meter race in 12.54 seconds.
   Which runner ran at a faster average rate?

   _____

7. Elmer Elementary School has 576 students
   and 24 teachers. Savoy Elementary School
   has 638 students and 29 teachers. Which
   school has the lower unit rate of students per
   teacher?

   _____

8. One cell phone company offers 500 minutes
   of talk time for $49.99. Another company
   offers 480 minutes for $44.99. Which
   company offers the better deal?

   _____

MIXED APPLICATIONS

9. Sylvio's flight is scheduled to travel 1,792
   miles in 3.5 hours. At what average rate will
   the plane have to travel to complete the trip
   on time?

   _____

10. Rachel bought 2 pounds of apples and 3
    pounds of peaches for a total of $10.45. The
    apples and peaches cost the same amount per
    pound. What was the unit rate?

   _____

Name _____   Date _____

Use Tables to Compare Ratios

Solve each problem.

1. Sarah asked some friends about their favorite colors. She found that 4 out of 6 people prefer blue, and 8 out of 12 people prefer green. Is the ratio of friends who chose blue to the total asked equivalent to the ratio of friends who chose green to the total asked?

Blue				
Friends who chose blue	4	8	12	16
Total asked	6	12	18	24

Green				
Friends who chose green	8	16	24	32
Total asked	12	24	36	48

2. Lisa and Tim make necklaces. Lisa uses 5 red beads for every 3 yellow beads. Tim uses 9 red beads for every 6 yellow beads. Is the ratio of red beads to yellow beads in Lisa's necklace equivalent to the ratio in Tim's necklace?

3. Mitch scored 4 out of 5 on a quiz. Demetri scored 8 out of 10 on a quiz. Did Mitch and Demetri get equivalent scores?

4. Chandra ordered 10 chicken nuggets and ate 7 of them. Raul ordered 15 chicken nuggets and ate 12 of them. Is Chandra's ratio of nuggets ordered to nuggets eaten equivalent to Raul's ratio of nuggets ordered to nuggets eaten?

82

Equivalent Ratios and Graphs

Use the following information to solve Exercises 1–4. Christie makes bracelets. She uses 8 charms for each bracelet.

1. Complete the table of equivalent ratios for the first 5 bracelets.

Charms					
Bracelets	1	2			

2. Write ordered pairs, letting the *x*-coordinate represent the number of bracelets and the *y*-coordinate represent the number of charms.

   (1, _____), (2, _____), (_____ , _____),

   (_____ , _____), (_____ , _____)

4. What does the point (1, 8) represent on the graph?

   _____

   _____

3. Use the ordered pairs to graph the charms and bracelets.

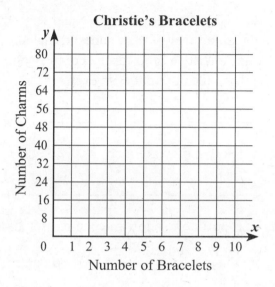

Christie's Bracelets

Use the graph to solve Exercises 5–6. The graph shows the number of granola bars that are in various numbers of boxes of Crunch N Go.

5. Complete the table of equivalent ratios.

Bars				
Boxes	1	2	3	4

6. Find the unit rate of granola bars per box.

   _____

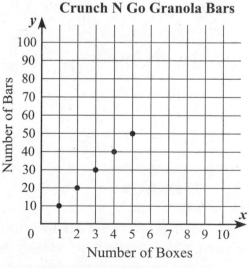

Crunch N Go Granola Bars

MIXED APPLICATIONS

7. Look at the graph for Christie's Bracelets. How many charms are needed for 7 bracelets?

   _____

8. Look at the graph for Crunch N Go Granola Bars. Stefan needs to buy 90 granola bars. How many boxes must he buy?

   _____

Exploring Proportions

Compare the number of light cubes to the number of dark cubes.

1. Write a ratio for the comparison.

_____

2. Separate the light cubes into two equal sets.
Put an equal number of dark cubes in each of
the two sets. Write a ratio for the comparison
of the light to the dark cubes in each set.

_____

3. How are the two ratios related?

_____

4. Write a proportion to show the comparison of the two ratios. _____

5. Compare the cross products of the two ratios. _____

**Look at these squares and circles. Write a ratio in
fraction form for each of the following comparisons.**

6. light squares to dark squares _____   **7.** light squares to light circles _____

8. dark squares to light squares _____   **9.** light circles to light squares _____

10. dark circles to light circles _____   **11.** dark circles to dark squares _____

VISUAL THINKING

12. Look at the diagram. Write a ratio in fraction
form for the comparison of triangles to rectangles.
(Hint: Remember to count triangles and rectangles
of all sizes.)

_____

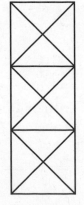

84

Name _____ Date _____

Use Unit Rates

Use a unit rate to find each unknown value.

1. $\dfrac{34}{17} = \dfrac{\square}{7}$

2. $\dfrac{16}{32} = \dfrac{\square}{14}$

3. $\dfrac{18}{\square} = \dfrac{21}{7}$

4. $\dfrac{\square}{16} = \dfrac{3}{12}$

_____   _____   _____   _____

Draw a bar model to find each unknown value.

5. $\dfrac{15}{45} = \dfrac{6}{\square}$

6. $\dfrac{3}{6} = \dfrac{\square}{7}$

_____   _____

7. $\dfrac{\square}{6} = \dfrac{6}{9}$

8. $\dfrac{7}{\square} = \dfrac{2}{10}$

_____   _____

MIXED APPLICATIONS

9. To stay properly hydrated, a person should drink 32 fluid ounces of water for every 60 minutes of exercise. How much water should Damon drink if he rides his bike for 135 minutes?

_____

10. Lillianne made 6 out of every 10 baskets she attempted during basketball practice. If she attempted to make 25 baskets, how many did she make?

_____

Problem-Solving Strategy

MAKE A TABLE

Make a table for each problem and then solve.

1. In January, canned apricots cost 68 cents. Canned peaches cost 78 cents. During the year, the price of apricots increased by 4 cents per month. The price of peaches increased by 2 cents per month. Find the month when both items sold for the same price.

   _____

2. Domingo had 250 baseball cards and Jennifer had 82 baseball cards. At the first meeting of the Card Club and at every meeting thereafter, Domingo sold 12 cards to Jennifer. After which meeting did the two have the same number of cards?

   _____

3. Stefan took a job at $23,000 the first year with annual raises of $1,090 thereafter. Brenda took a job at $24,020 a year with annual raises of $950 thereafter. During which year will Stefan start earning more than Brenda?

   _____

4. In November, the Sport Shop sold 74 pairs of snow skis and 3 pairs of water skis. Each month the shop sold 11 more pairs of water skis and 6 fewer pairs of snow skis than the previous month. When was the first month the shop sold more water skis than snow skis?

   _____

5. Briana tore a sheet of paper in half. Then she tore each of the remaining pieces in half. She continued this process 6 more times. How many pieces of paper did she have at the end?

   _____

6. Mr. Hassan's house number is composed of 3 consecutive digits. It is a multiple of his age, which is 63. What is Mr. Hassan's house number?

   _____

Introduction to Percent

Write a fraction, a decimal, and a percent for each shaded region.

1.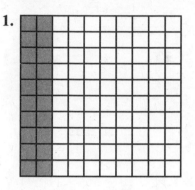

2.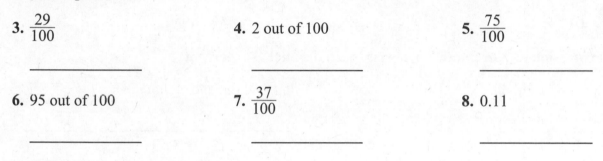

_____   _____

Write as a percent.

3. $\frac{29}{100}$

4. 2 out of 100

5. $\frac{75}{100}$

_____   _____   _____

6. 95 out of 100

7. $\frac{37}{100}$

8. 0.11

_____   _____   _____

MIXED APPLICATIONS

9. Larry is correct 54% of the time in his weather prediction. Express this percent as a fraction and as a decimal.

_____

10. Tomatoes are on sale for 3 lb for $1.09. How much will 5 lb of tomatoes cost?

_____

VISUAL THINKING

11. Look at the grids. What percent of each grid is shaded?

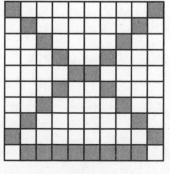 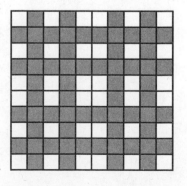

Connecting Percents and Decimals

Write each percent as a decimal.

1. 85% _____

2. 3% _____

3. 95% _____

4. 17% _____

5. 68% _____

6. 16.2% _____

7. 4% _____

8. 155% _____

9. 50% _____

10. 71.5% _____

11. 88.8% _____

12. 103% _____

Write each decimal as a percent.

13. 0.06 _____

14. 0.78 _____

15. 1.43 _____

16. 0.607 _____

17. 0.52 _____

18. 0.11 _____

19. 1.09 _____

20. 1.406 _____

21. 1.65 _____

Write each expression as a decimal. Then write each decimal as a percent.

22. ten and twelve hundredths

23. thirty-seven and eight tenths

_____

_____

MIXED APPLICATIONS

24. The sale price of a TV was 82% of the original amount. Write the percent as a decimal.

25. Pedro travels 286 mi in 4 hr 24 min. At this rate, how far will Pedro travel in 5 hr 24 min?

_____

_____

NUMBER SENSE

26. The quotient $\frac{5}{7} \div \frac{15}{28}$ is $\frac{4}{3}$. Use 5, 7, 15, and 28 to write two other fractions that have a quotient of $\frac{4}{3}$ and two fractions that have a quotient of $\frac{3}{4}$.

_____

88

Name _____ Date _____

Connecting Percents and Fractions

Write each percent as a mixed number or as a fraction in simplest form.

1. 71% _____

2. 3% _____

3. 410% _____

4. 160% _____

5. 56% _____

6. 66% _____

7. 78% _____

8. 84% _____

9. 28% _____

Write each fraction as a percent.

10. $\frac{11}{100}$ _____

11. $\frac{3}{4}$ _____

12. $\frac{63}{100}$ _____

13. $\frac{7}{10}$ _____

14. $\frac{48}{25}$ _____

15. $\frac{97}{100}$ _____

16. $\frac{700}{1,000}$ _____

17. $\frac{5}{8}$ _____

18. $\frac{22}{25}$ _____

MIXED APPLICATIONS

19. About $\frac{4}{5}$ of the volume of Earth's atmosphere is nitrogen. What percent is this?

_____

20. Nakano's Car Sales increased its sales of sedans by 18%. By what fraction did the company increase its sales?

_____

21. About 21% of Earth's atmosphere is oxygen. Write this percent as a fraction.

_____

22. About 0.03 of Earth's water is fresh water. What percent is this?

_____

MIXED REVIEW

Tell whether the ratios are equivalent. Write *yes* or *no*.

23. $\frac{5}{7}$; $\frac{15}{21}$ _____

24. $\frac{3}{4}$; $\frac{27}{32}$ _____

25. 8:10; 24:30 _____

26. 10:20; 60:180 _____

Find each unit rate or unit price.

27. 7 for $2.10 _____

28. $400 for 8 hours of work _____

29. 504 mi per 12 gal _____

30. 40 hr for $460 _____

Unit 10
Core Skills Math, Grade 6

Understanding Percent

Write each as a percent.

1. 85 out of 100 _____   **2.** 42 out of 100 _____   **3.** 12 per 100 _____

4. 9 per 100 _____   **5.** 93 out of 100 _____   **6.** 79 per 100 _____

7. $\frac{3}{100}$ _____   **8.** $\frac{97}{100}$ _____   **9.** $\frac{49}{100}$ _____   **10.** 53:100 _____

11. $\frac{3}{20}$ _____   **12.** $\frac{1}{2}$ _____   **13.** $\frac{5}{25}$ _____   **14.** $\frac{2}{1}$ _____

15. $\frac{3}{4}$ _____   **16.** $\frac{9}{10}$ _____   **17.** $\frac{18}{50}$ _____   **18.** $\frac{4}{25}$ _____

19. $\frac{1}{20}$ _____   **20.** $\frac{167}{100}$ _____   **21.** $\frac{2}{5}$ _____   **22.** $\frac{17}{8}$ _____

MIXED APPLICATIONS

23. The owner of Tourist T-shirts sold 80 T-shirts today. The owner calculated that $\frac{3}{4}$ of those T-shirts were size large. What percent of the T-shirts sold were size large?

_____

24. The owner of Tourist T-shirts sells about $\frac{3}{5}$ of his T-shirts to teenagers. What percent of his T-shirts are sold to teenagers?

_____

25. Last month $\frac{1}{10}$ of the T-shirts sold were size extra-large and $\frac{1}{8}$ were size extra-small. Were more extra-large or extra-small T-shirts sold last month?

_____

26. During the month of July, $\frac{3}{20}$ of the T-shirts sold were size small and $\frac{10}{25}$ of the T-shirts sold were size large. What percent of the T-shirts sold were neither small nor large?

_____

VISUAL THINKING

27. What percent of the large square is shaded? Explain your reasoning.

_____

_____

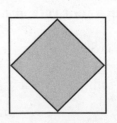

90

Exploring Percent of a Number

1. How can you express 14% as a decimal? _____

2. How can you express 8% as a fraction? _____

Use a decimal to find the percent of each number.

3. 30% of 60 _____   **4.** 50% of 40 _____   **5.** 40% of 100 _____

6. 80% of 130 _____   **7.** 90% of 350 _____   **8.** 60% of 30 _____

9. 70% of 150 _____   **10.** 20% of 600 _____   **11.** 10% of 70 _____

12. 3% of 600 _____   **13.** 400% of 2 _____   **14.** 9% of 20,000 _____

Use a fraction to find the percent of each number.

15. 10% of 80 _____   **16.** 50% of 120 _____   **17.** 25% of 44 _____

18. 75% of 24 _____   **19.** 90% of 30 _____   **20.** 80% of 140 _____

21. 25% of 84 _____   **22.** 75% of 100 _____   **23.** 40% of 20 _____

24. 30% of 600 _____   **25.** 45% of 20 _____   **26.** 65% of 200 _____

Use a calculator to find the percent of each number.

27. 15% of 45 _____   **28.** 3% of 420 _____   **29.** 45% of 160 _____

30. 12% of 65 _____   **31.** 15% of 70 _____   **32.** 68% of 68 _____

33. 24% of 700 _____   **34.** 28% of 180 _____   **35.** 55% of 680 _____

36. 56% of 20 _____   **37.** 33% of 270 _____   **38.** 66% of 360 _____

EVERYDAY MATH CONNECTION

39. List three everyday situations in which you need to find the percent of a number.

_____

_____

Mental Math and Percent

Use mental math to find the percent of each number.

1. 20% of 400 _____

2. 5% of 300 _____

3. 15% of 600 _____

4. 30% of 40 _____

5. 50% of 200 _____

6. 10% of 14 _____

7. 8% of 400 _____

8. 100% of 45 _____

9. 10% of 5 _____

10. 25% of $3.20 _____

11. 200% of 10 _____

12. 50% of $4.20 _____

13. 75% of $40 _____

14. 100% of $3.56 _____

15. 10% of $45.60 _____

16. 25% of 400 _____

17. 55% of 200 _____

18. 35% of 40 _____

MIXED APPLICATIONS

19. Sue got 48 out of 60 questions correct on a quiz. What percent score did she get?

_____

20. Of 1,200 people surveyed, 44% preferred rail to air travel. How many people preferred rail travel?

_____

21. Martha wants to arrange 20 cassettes in equal stacks. How many cassettes can Martha put in each stack?

_____

22. Matt made 15 birthday cards. He gave 40% of the cards to his friends. How many cards did he give to his friends?

_____

MIXED REVIEW

Find each unit rate.

23. 3 pillows for $45

24. 75 pages in 5 h

25. 525 mi per 21 gal

_____   _____   _____

Tell whether the ratios make a proportion. Write *yes* or *no*.

26. $\frac{1}{2}$; $\frac{4}{8}$ _____

27. $\frac{2}{3}$; $\frac{8}{9}$ _____

28. $\frac{28}{49}$; $\frac{4}{7}$ _____

29. $\frac{6}{7}$; $\frac{12}{21}$ _____

Write as a percent.

30. 0.45 _____

31. $\frac{3}{5}$ _____

32. 0.66

33. $\frac{1}{4}$ _____

Percent of a Number

Find the percent of each number.

1. 6% of 20 _____

2. 85% of 150 _____

3. 25% of 60 _____

4. 75% of 96 _____

5. 56% of 120 _____

6. 45% of 84 _____

7. 30% of 45 _____

8. 70% of 148 _____

9. 2% of 63 _____

Solve.

10. What number is 14% of 70?

_____

11. What number is 81% of 40?

_____

12. 75% of 240 is what number?

_____

13. 200% of $35 is what amount?

_____

14. What number is 26% of 130?

_____

15. What number is 1.7% of 19?

_____

MIXED APPLICATIONS

16. In 1965 a dress cost $30.00. Fifteen years later, the price had increased by 15%. How much more did it sell for fifteen years later?

_____

17. How much farther does a bicycle tire with a 30-in. diameter roll in one revolution than a tire with a 21-in. diameter? Hint: $C = \pi d$

_____

BUSINESS CONNECTION

Solve.

Stockbrokers charge a fee for handling the sale of stock for an investor. Assume that a broker's fee is 1.5% of the sale price. Find the amount that the investor receives. Round to the next cent when necessary.

18. sale of 20 shares of Doublestock Publishing at $24 per share

_____

19. sale of 50 shares of Angel Air at $10\frac{1}{2} per share

_____

Name _____ Date _____

Percents and Proportions

Solve. You may use either the proportion method or the equation method.

1. 40% of what number is 16?

_____

2. 15% of what number is 75?

_____

3. 8 is 20% of what number?

_____

4. 18 is 9% of what number?

_____

5. 25% of what number is 14?

_____

6. 9% of what number is 54?

_____

7. 6 is 50% of what number?

_____

8. 67 is 67% of what number?

_____

9. 270 is 54% of what number?

_____

10. 2% of what number is 32?

_____

MIXED APPLICATIONS

11. Casey earned $14,760 this year. This year's salary is 123% of last year's salary. How much did he earn last year?

_____

12. Aretha figured a 15% tip on a $5.40 lunch bill. She rounded the tip up to the next multiple of 5 cents. What was the amount of Aretha's tip?

_____

BUSINESS CONNECTION

Solve.

Many stores sell items at a percentage discount (discount rate). The sale price is the original price minus the discount. Find the discount and the sale price.

13. Original price: $15.50

   Discount rate: 10%

   Discount _____

   Sale Price _____

14. Original price: $32.00

   Discount rate: 50%

   Discount _____

   Sale Price _____

© Houghton Mifflin Harcourt Publishing Company

Estimating Percents

Choose the best estimate. Circle *a*, *b*, or *c*.

1. 61% of 50
   a. 20
   b. 25
   c. 30

2. 31% of $89
   a. $10
   b. $20
   c. $30

3. 67% of 211
   a. 140
   b. 150
   c. 180

Estimate each percent.

4. $\frac{64}{124}$ _____

5. $\frac{7}{25}$ _____

6. $\frac{9}{32}$ _____

7. 6 out of 49 _____

8. 42 out of 117 _____

9. 21 out of 81 _____

10. $\frac{33}{60}$ _____

11. $\frac{79}{155}$ _____

12. $\frac{165}{320}$ _____

Estimate each number.

13. 51 is 25% of what number?

14. 8 is 9% of what number?

MIXED APPLICATIONS

15. Juan paid $59.99 for a jacket that originally sold for $85.50. About what percent of the original price did he pay for the jacket?

16. In a circle graph showing audience share for 5 different programs, the central angle for program A is 54°. What percent of the audience does program A have?

17. Of an order of bracelets, 63, or 84% of the total, arrived. What is the total number of bracelets ordered?

NUMBER SENSE

18. Dawn bought a book at a 35% discount. She paid $18.20. What was the original price?

Exploring Percent Problems

Complete to solve the following problem:

1. The Hat Hut sold 30 hats this morning. This was 40% of the number of hats it sold all day. How many hats did the Hat Hut sell today?

   Think: 40% of ☐ = _____

   $\dfrac{40}{100} = \dfrac{30}{75}$

   So, the Hat Hut sold _____ hats today.

Choose the correct percent problem for each word problem. Write _a_, _b_, or _c_ on the blank line.

2. Bill had 50 baseball cards. He traded 20% of the cards with his friend Sam. How many baseball cards did he trade with Sam?

   a. ☐% of 20 = 50   **b.** 20% of ☐ = 50   **c.** 20% of 50 = ☐

   _____

3. Aimee had $10 in her wallet. She spent $4 on school supplies. What percent of her money did she spend on school supplies?

   a. ☐% of 10 = 4   **b.** 4% of 10 = ☐   **c.** 4% of ☐ = 10

   _____

4. Twelve students were chosen to act in a school play. This was 40% of the number of students who auditioned for the play. How many students auditioned for the play?

   a. ☐% of 40 = 12   **b.** 40% of ☐ = 12   **c.** 40% of 12 = ☐

   _____

5. Tom had $60 in his savings account. He withdrew 10% of his savings to pay a debt to his sister. How much money did he withdraw from his savings account?

   a. 10% of 60 = ☐   **b.** 10% of ☐ = 60   **c.** ☐% of 60 = 10

   _____

WRITER'S CORNER

6. Write a word problem that can be solved by the percent problem ☐ of 85 = 51.

   _____

   _____

Finding the Number When the Percent Is Known

Find each number.

1. 85% of what number is 68? _____

2. 24 is 15% of what number? _____

3. 136.8 is 19% of what number? _____

4. 37% of what number is 74? _____

5. 0.6% of what number is 1.14? _____

6. 96% of what number is 192? _____

7. 145 is 58% of what number? _____

8. 0.25 is 0.05% of what number? _____

9. 4% of what number is 26.8? _____

10. 130% of what number is 75.4? _____

11. 24.6 is 24% of what number? _____

12. 75% of what number is 75? _____

13. 84% of what number is 210? _____

14. 0.98 is 35% of what number? _____

15. 5 is 0.2% of what number? _____

16. 35% of what number is 43.75? _____

17. 56% of what number is 39.2? _____

18. 11% of what number is 24.2? _____

MIXED APPLICATIONS

19. By next year, 2,125 students are expected to be enrolled in a county's middle schools. This is 25% of the total student population. What is the total student population?

    _____

20. On a business trip, Ms. Rupp drove 4.25 hr on Monday, 6.75 hr on Tuesday, 5.5 hr on Wednesday, 7 hr on Thursday, and 6.75 hr on Friday. What is the total number of hours that Ms. Rupp drove?

    _____

MIXED REVIEW

Solve each proportion.

21. $\frac{1}{10} = \frac{12}{n}$ _____

22. $\frac{2}{3} = \frac{n}{9}$ _____

23. $\frac{4}{n} = \frac{20}{250}$ _____

Find the percent of each number.

24. 25% of 90 _____

25. 10% of 87.2 _____

26. 3% of 42 _____

Area of Rectangles

Find each area.

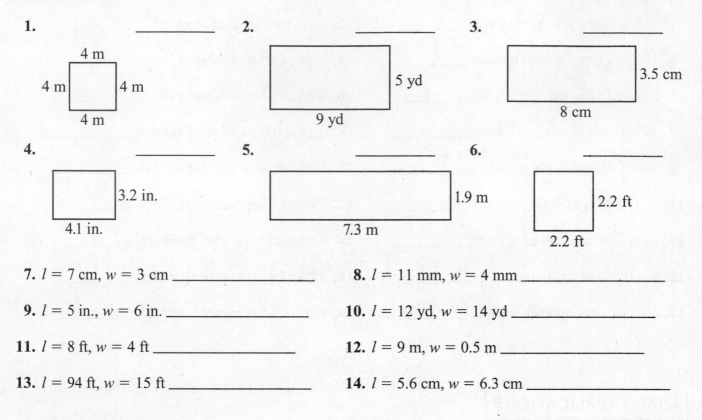

1. _____
4 m
4 m | 4 m
4 m

2. _____
5 yd
9 yd

3. _____
3.5 cm
8 cm

4. _____
3.2 in.
4.1 in.

5. _____
1.9 m
7.3 m

6. _____
2.2 ft
2.2 ft

7. $l = 7$ cm, $w = 3$ cm _____

8. $l = 11$ mm, $w = 4$ mm _____

9. $l = 5$ in., $w = 6$ in. _____

10. $l = 12$ yd, $w = 14$ yd _____

11. $l = 8$ ft, $w = 4$ ft _____

12. $l = 9$ m, $w = 0.5$ m _____

13. $l = 94$ ft, $w = 15$ ft _____

14. $l = 5.6$ cm, $w = 6.3$ cm _____

MIXED APPLICATIONS

15. The length of a rug is 3 yards. The width is 2 yards. What is the area of the rug?

_____

16. Vanessa's room is 15 feet long and 12 feet wide. What is the area of her room?

_____

17. A rug is 10 ft long and 8 ft wide. What is the perimeter of the rug?

_____

18. A carpet costs $8.95 per square yard. What is the cost of carpeting for a room 12 feet long and 9 feet wide?

_____

NUMBER SENSE

19. The area of a rectangle is 27 cm². If the width is 3 cm, what is the length?

_____

20. The area of a rectangle is 4 ft². If the length is 5 ft, what is the width?

_____

98

Find Area Using a Grid

Find the area of each figure.

1.

4 cm
3 cm

_____

2.

4 cm
2 cm

_____

3.

4 mi
4 mi

_____

4.

6 m
3 m

_____

5.

2 cm
4 cm

_____

6.

7 ft
3 ft

_____

7. parallelogram

$b = 7$ in.

$h = 9$ in.

_____

8. triangle

$b = 12$ m

$h = 8$ m

_____

9. parallelogram

$b = 5$ ft

$h = 17$ ft

_____

MIXED APPLICATIONS

10. A rectangular mirror is 14 in. wide and 23 in. long. What is the area of the mirror?

_____

11. A park is in the shape of a triangle with a base 120 m and height 48 m. What is the area of the park?

_____

LOGICAL REASONING

12. Without calculating, decide which has the greater area: a triangle with a base of 7 m and a height of 12 m or a parallelogram with a base of 7 m and a height of 5 m. Explain your answer.

_____

_____

Name _____ Date _____

Area of Parallelograms and Triangles

Find the area of each parallelogram.

1. $b = 4$ cm, $h = 6$ cm _____ **2.** $b = 14$ ft, $h = 20$ ft _____

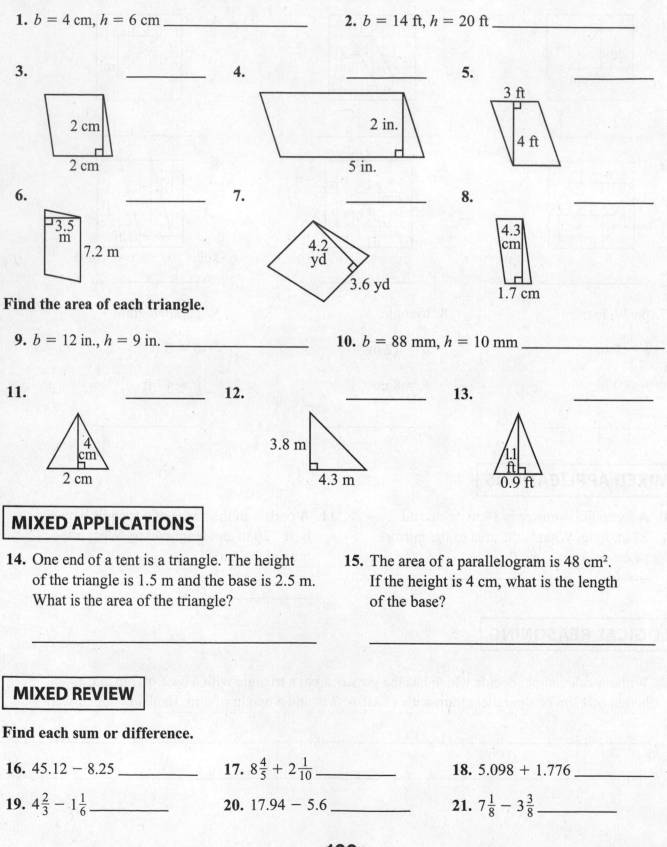

3. _____

4. _____

5. _____

6. _____

7. _____

8. _____

Find the area of each triangle.

9. $b = 12$ in., $h = 9$ in. _____ **10.** $b = 88$ mm, $h = 10$ mm _____

11. _____

12. _____

13. _____

MIXED APPLICATIONS

14. One end of a tent is a triangle. The height of the triangle is 1.5 m and the base is 2.5 m. What is the area of the triangle?

_____

15. The area of a parallelogram is 48 cm². If the height is 4 cm, what is the length of the base?

_____

MIXED REVIEW

Find each sum or difference.

16. $45.12 - 8.25$ _____

17. $8\frac{4}{5} + 2\frac{1}{10}$ _____

18. $5.098 + 1.776$ _____

19. $4\frac{2}{3} - 1\frac{1}{6}$ _____

20. $17.94 - 5.6$ _____

21. $7\frac{1}{8} - 3\frac{3}{8}$ _____

100

Problem-Solving Strategy

USE A FORMULA

Solve.

1. Mrs. Taylor's art class made a banner to hang on the gym wall. If the banner is 30 feet long and 3 feet wide, how much of the wall does the banner cover?

   _____

2. The school parking lot is rectangular. The area of the parking lot is 2,750 m². If the length of the parking lot is 55 m, what is the width?

   _____

Choose a strategy and solve.

3. Wanda jogs along a rectangular path. She always jogs east, then south, then west, then north. If she jogs 2 mi east and 3 mi south, how far does she jog?

   _____

4. Devon can buy 6 skeins of yarn for $8.10. If she needs 15 skeins for a project, how much will she spend on yarn?

   _____

5. Lillian drives to work at an average speed of 45 miles per hour. If she travels 30 miles to work and leaves at 8:00 A.M., at what time does she get to work?

   _____

6. Roberto gave 16 baseball cards to his friends. If he kept $\frac{3}{4}$ of his baseball cards, how many cards did he have in the beginning?

   _____

WRITER'S CORNER

7. Write a problem that involves making a banner and can be solved using a formula.

   _____

   _____

   _____

Finding Area: Complex and Curved Figures

Find the area of each complex figure.

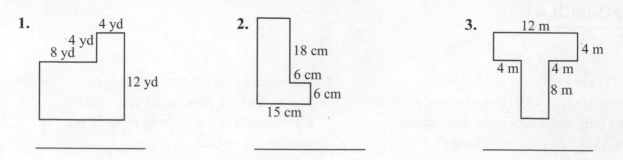

1.
4 yd
4 yd
8 yd
12 yd

_____

2.
18 cm
6 cm
6 cm
15 cm

_____

3.
12 m
4 m
4 m   4 m
8 m

_____

Estimate the area of each shaded region.

4.

_____

5.

_____

MIXED APPLICATIONS

6. A circle is drawn on a piece of 1-cm graph paper. It covers 20 squares and 6 partial squares. Estimate the area of the circle.

_____

7. Joy's backyard measures 25 ft by 40 ft. Sofia's backyard measures 30 by 30 ft. Who has a bigger yard and by how much?

_____

NUMBER SENSE

8. The shaded figure fits completely inside the triangle. Can the shaded figure have a greater area than the triangle? Can it have a greater perimeter than the triangle? Give reasons for your answers.

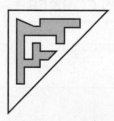

_____

_____

_____

Area of Rectangles and Parallelograms

Find the area of each polygon.

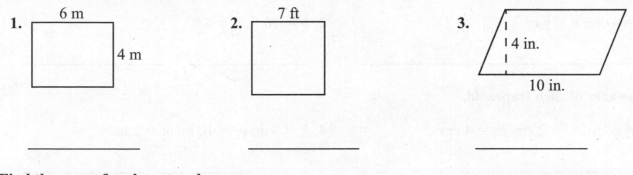

1. 6 m
    4 m

2. 7 ft

3. 4 in.
    10 in.

_____ _____ _____

Find the area of each rectangle.

4. $l = 6$ in., $w = 3$ in.

5. $l = 12$ m, $w = 8$ m

6. $l = 9.4$ m, $w = 6.7$ m

_____ _____ _____

Find the area of the shaded region of each figure.

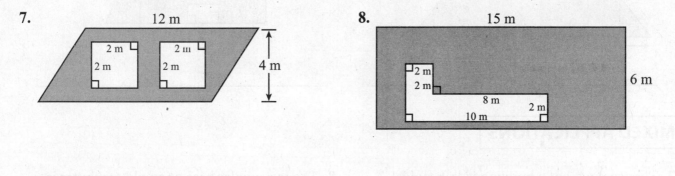

7. 12 m
    2 m   2 m
    2 m   2 m
    4 m

8. 15 m
    2 m
    2 m
    8 m   2 m
    10 m   6 m

_____ _____

MIXED APPLICATIONS

9. A rectangular pan is 10 in. wide and has a length of 14 in. What is the area of the pan?

_____

10. Mr. Santiago bought a rug with an area of 2,500 sq. in. Will the rug fit in the front hall, which is 48 in. by 60 in.?

_____

SOCIAL STUDIES CONNECTION

11. The state of Wyoming is roughly rectangular in shape. It has an area of more than 96,000 square miles. Write some possible dimensions of the state's length and width.

_____

Area of Triangles and Trapezoids

Find the area of each triangle.

1. $b = 4$ cm, $h = 6$ cm

   _____

2. $b = 10$ ft, $h = 5$ ft

   _____

Find the area of each trapezoid.

3. $h = 6$ cm, $b_1 = 2$ cm, $b_2 = 4$ cm

   _____

4. $h = 9$ m, $b_1 = 10$ m, $b_2 = 2$ m

   _____

Find the area of each shaded region.

5.

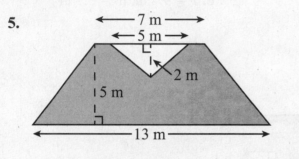

6.

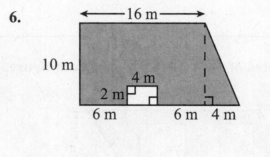

MIXED APPLICATIONS

7. The front wall of a building is trapezoidal in shape. Its bases are 12 m and 14 m. The height of the building is 10 m. What is the area of the front wall?

   _____

8. The rectangular base of an old computer is 1 ft by 2 ft. The area of the base of the monitor that goes with the computer is 4 ft². What is the total area occupied by both the base of the computer and the monitor?

   _____

ART CONNECTION

9. Make a design composed of triangles and trapezoids. Make the measure of each side of each figure a whole number. Calculate the area of the entire drawing.

Exploring Surface Area

Answer the questions to find the surface area of the pyramid in Figure A.

The square-based pyramid in Figure A has a base that is 5 cm square.
The sides are isosceles triangles with heights of 5 cm.

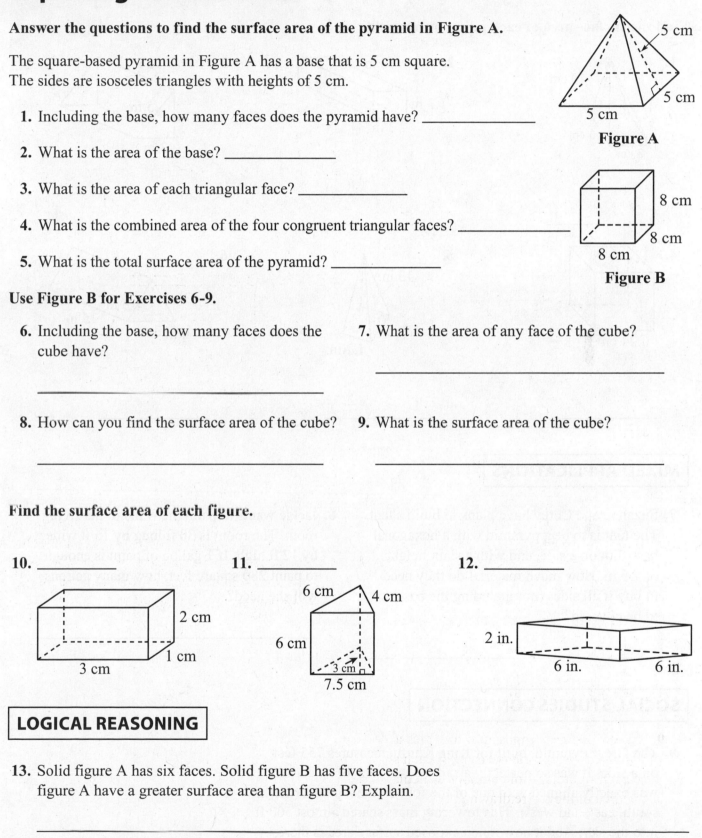

Figure A

1. Including the base, how many faces does the pyramid have? _____

2. What is the area of the base? _____

3. What is the area of each triangular face? _____

4. What is the combined area of the four congruent triangular faces? _____

5. What is the total surface area of the pyramid? _____

Figure B

Use Figure B for Exercises 6–9.

6. Including the base, how many faces does the cube have?

   _____

7. What is the area of any face of the cube?

   _____

8. How can you find the surface area of the cube?

   _____

9. What is the surface area of the cube?

   _____

Find the surface area of each figure.

10. _____

11. _____

12. _____

LOGICAL REASONING

13. Solid figure A has six faces. Solid figure B has five faces. Does
    figure A have a greater surface area than figure B? Explain.

    _____

    _____

Surface Area of Prisms and Pyramids

Find the surface area of each prism or pyramid.

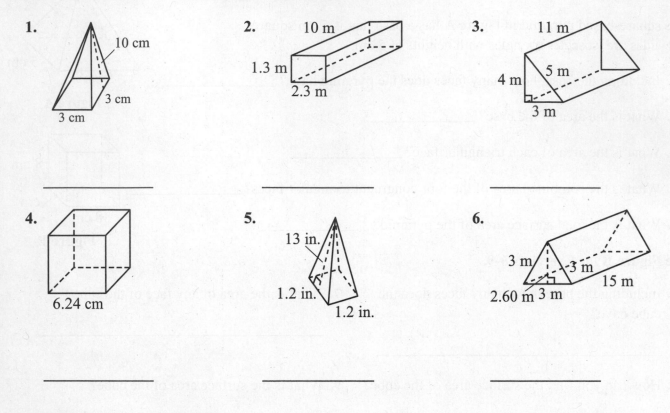

1.   10 cm
     3 cm
     3 cm

_____

2.   10 m
     1.3 m
     2.3 m

_____

3.   11 m
     5 m
     4 m
     3 m

_____

4.   6.24 cm

_____

5.   13 in.
     1.2 in.
     1.2 in.

_____

6.   3 m
     3 m
     15 m
     2.60 m   3 m

_____

MIXED APPLICATIONS

7. Suzanne and Corey have plans to build a tent. The tent is to be a pyramid with a hexagonal base 3 m on a side, and with a slant height of 7.5 m. How much material do they need to buy if all sides (not including the base) are to be covered?

_____

8. Jackie wants to paint the walls of her living room. The room is 30 ft long by 15 ft wide by 12 ft high. If 1 gallon of paint is enough to paint 280 square feet, how many gallons will she need?

_____

SOCIAL STUDIES CONNECTION

9. The Great Pyramid, built for King Khufu, measures 755 feet on a side. It was so perfectly arranged that each of its corners was exactly aligned with one of the four cardinal points (north, south, east, and west). This towering mass soared almost 500 ft into the sky. About how much exposed surface area is there, assuming the surfaces are flat? (HINT: slant height = 626.5 feet.)

_____

106

Fractions and Volume

Find the volume of each rectangular prism.

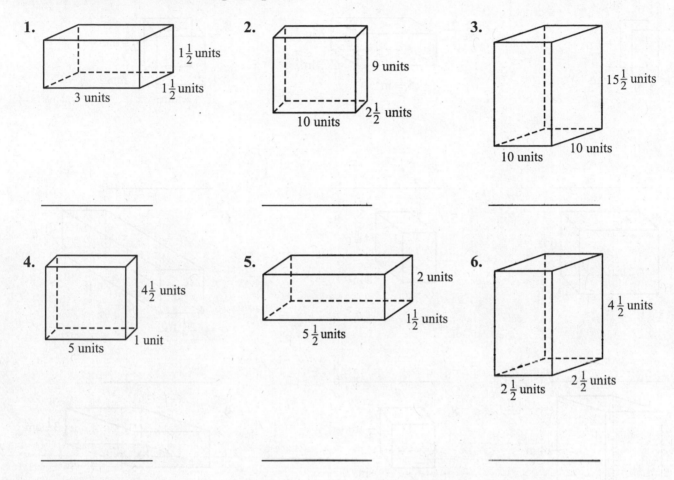

1.

$1\frac{1}{2}$ units

$1\frac{1}{2}$ units

3 units

_____

2.

9 units

$2\frac{1}{2}$ units

10 units

_____

3.

$15\frac{1}{2}$ units

10 units   10 units

_____

4.

$4\frac{1}{2}$ units

5 units   1 unit

_____

5.

2 units

$1\frac{1}{2}$ units

$5\frac{1}{2}$ units

_____

6.

$4\frac{1}{2}$ units

$2\frac{1}{2}$ units $2\frac{1}{2}$ units

_____

MIXED APPLICATIONS

7. Miguel is pouring liquid into a container that is $4\frac{1}{2}$ inches long by $3\frac{1}{2}$ inches wide by 2 inches high. How many cubic inches of liquid will fit in the container?

_____

8. A shipping crate is shaped like a rectangular prism. It is $5\frac{1}{2}$ feet long by 3 feet wide by 3 feet high. What is the volume of the crate?

_____

Volume of Rectangular Prisms

Find the volume of each prism.

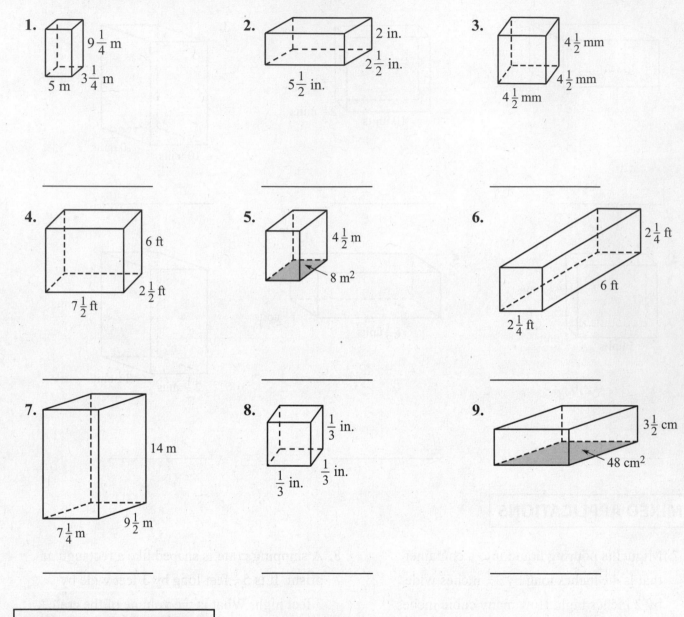

1. $9\frac{1}{4}$ m $3\frac{1}{4}$ m   5 m

2. 2 in. $2\frac{1}{2}$ in. $5\frac{1}{2}$ in.

3. $4\frac{1}{2}$ mm $4\frac{1}{2}$ mm $4\frac{1}{2}$ mm

4. 6 ft $2\frac{1}{2}$ ft $7\frac{1}{2}$ ft

5. $4\frac{1}{2}$ m   8 m^2

6. $2\frac{1}{4}$ ft   6 ft $2\frac{1}{4}$ ft

7. 14 m $9\frac{1}{2}$ m $7\frac{1}{4}$ m

8. $\frac{1}{3}$ in. $\frac{1}{3}$ in. $\frac{1}{3}$ in.

9. $3\frac{1}{2}$ cm   48 cm^2

MIXED APPLICATIONS

10. A cereal box is a rectangular prism that is 8 inches long and $2\frac{1}{2}$ inches wide. The volume of the box is 200 in.^{3}. What is the height of the box?

_____

11. A stack of paper is $8\frac{1}{2}$ in. long by 11 in. wide by 4 in. high. What is the volume of the stack of paper?

_____

    Unit 11
Core Skills Math, Grade 6

Name _____ Date _____

Understanding Positive and Negative Numbers

Graph each integer and its opposite on a number line.

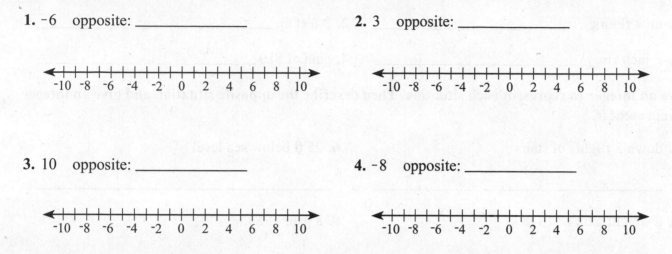

1. ⁻6   opposite: _____

2. 3   opposite: _____

3. 10   opposite: _____

4. ⁻8   opposite: _____

Name the integer that represents each situation and tell what 0 represents in that situation.

	Situation	Integer	What Does 0 Represent?
5.	Michael withdrew $60 from his checking account.		
6.	Raquel gained 12 points while playing a video game.		
7.	Juan went up 25 feet during a climb on a rock climbing wall.		

Write the opposite of each integer.

8. ⁻20 _____   9. 4 _____   10. 95 _____   11. ⁻63 _____

MIXED APPLICATIONS

12. Dakshesh won a game by scoring 25 points. Randy scored the opposite number of points as Dakshesh. What is Randy's score?

13. When Dakshesh and Randy played the game again, Dakshesh scored the opposite of the opposite of his first score. What is his score?

Integers

Describe the opposite of each situation.

1. up 4 floors _____

2. 8 feet up _____

3. 2-inch rise _____

4. gain of $10 _____

Give an integer to represent each situation. Then describe the opposite situation and give an integer to represent it.

5. down 3 flights of stairs

   _____

6. 25 ft below sea level

   _____

7. a weight gain of 10 lb

   _____

8. a gain of $45

   _____

9. 8 degrees below zero

   _____

10. climb up 6 m

    _____

MIXED APPLICATIONS

11. The stock market was up 8 points. What number would show this? What number would show the stock market down 8 points?

    _____

12. If the temperature rises 5° and later drops 5°, what is the new temperature?

    _____

13. A stock market report showed this pattern: +8, -2, +6, -4, +4, -6. If the pattern continues, what would the next two reports be?

    _____

14. Death Valley, California, is two hundred eighty-two feet below sea level. Write the elevation as an integer.

    _____

MIXED REVIEW

Find each product or quotient.

15. $\frac{2}{3} \times \frac{9}{12}$ _____

16. $\frac{3}{5} \div \frac{2}{15}$ _____

17. $2\frac{3}{4} \times 1\frac{1}{11}$ _____

Write each number either as a percent or a decimal.

18. 0.63 _____

19. $\frac{1}{2}$ _____

20. 7% _____

Name _____   Date _____

Comparing and Ordering Integers

Use the number line. Write an integer for each given point.

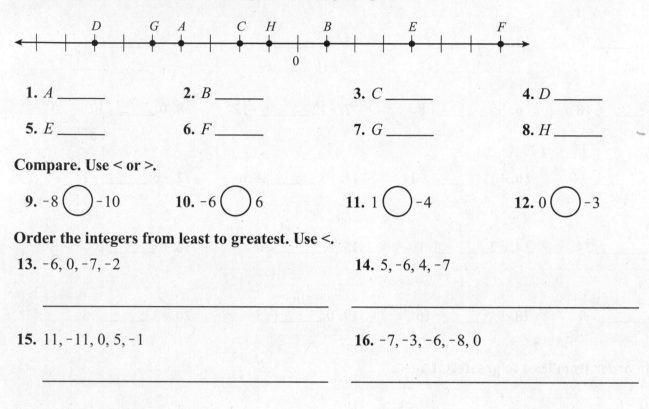

1. A _____   2. B _____   3. C _____   4. D _____

5. E _____   6. F _____   7. G _____   8. H _____

Compare. Use < or >.

9. -8 ◯ -10   10. -6 ◯ 6   11. 1 ◯ -4   12. 0 ◯ -3

Order the integers from least to greatest. Use <.

13. -6, 0, -7, -2

14. 5, -6, 4, -7

15. 11, -11, 0, 5, -1

16. -7, -3, -6, -8, 0

MIXED APPLICATIONS

17. Ponca City reports a temperature of 3° below zero. Marshall City reports a temperature of 5° below zero. Which city has the lower temperature?

18. Mr. Walker's house is on land that is 10 ft below sea level. Mr. Molina's house is on land that is 5 ft below sea level. Whose house is closer to sea level?

NUMBER SENSE

19. Whitney says she is thinking of two integers that are opposites. She says that there are 6 units between the two integers on the number line. What integers has Whitney chosen?

Compare and Order Integers Using Symbols

Compare. Write <, >, or =.

1. -9 _____ 7

2. -6 _____ 1

3. 8 _____ 8

4. 0 _____ -4

5. 31 _____ 18

6. -5 _____ -8

7. -12 _____ -12

8. 0 _____ 17

9. -13 _____ -9

10. -11 _____ -11

11. -3 _____ 2

12. -6 _____ -2

13. 45 _____ 54

14. -2 _____ -19

15. 6 _____ -6

16. 0 _____ 0

17. -1 _____ -1

18. 9 _____ -16

19. 0 _____ -5

20. -3 _____ -3

Write in order from least to greatest. Use <.

21. 5, 0, -6 _____

22. 17, 18, -20 _____

23. 0, -47, 74 _____

24. -4, 4, -6 _____

Write in order from greatest to least. Use >.

25. 1, -6, 8 _____

26. -13, -31, 44 _____

27. -2, -9, 0 _____

28. 7, -5, 0 _____

Understanding Numbers and Absolute Value

Write the absolute value of each number.

1. $|-7|$ _____   2. $|0|$ _____   3. $|-17|$ _____   4. $|22|$ _____

5. $|6|$ _____   6. $|-9|$ _____   7. $|-8|$ _____   8. $|13|$ _____

9. $|-12|$ _____   10. $|-19|$ _____   11. $|-11|$ _____   12. $|26|$ _____

13. $|18|$ _____   14. $|-3|$ _____   15. $|10|$ _____   16. $|-15|$ _____

Name the two numbers that have the given absolute value.

17. 23 _____   18. 14 _____

19. 32 _____   20. 29 _____

21. 21 _____   22. 40 _____

23. 12 _____   24. 99 _____

Name _____ Date _____

Understanding Integers

Write an integer for each description.

1. 27° below zero _____   **2.** a deposit of $20 _____   **3.** a loss of 4 lb _____

Write each absolute value.

4. |−4| _____   **5.** |−55| _____   **6.** |143| _____   **7.** |0| _____

Write the opposite of each number or situation.

8. −91 _____   **9.** −234 _____   **10.** 145 _____   **11.** −81 _____

12. biking east 3 km   **13.** spending $25   **14.** rising 5°C

_____   _____   _____

Compare. Write <, >, or =.

15. 10 ◯ 20   **16.** −4 ◯ −7   **17.** −10 ◯ −6   **18.** |5| ◯ |−5|

Order the integers from least to greatest.

19. 2, −3, −5, 3   **20.** 17, −17, −5, −2   **21.** 2, 5, −7, 4, −10

_____   _____   _____

MIXED APPLICATIONS

22. What two integers represent 20 degrees above zero and 20 degrees below zero?

_____

23. The change in temperature from noon to 6:00 P.M. was 5°C. The change in temperature from 6:00 P.M. to midnight was −8°C. Which time period had the greater change in temperature?

_____

SCIENCE CONNECTION

24. Zero degrees Celsius is equal to 273.15 degrees Kelvin. A change of 1 degree Celsius is equal to a change of 1 degree Kelvin. If zero degrees Kelvin is absolute zero, what integer would represent absolute zero on the Celsius scale?

_____

Unit 12
Core Skills Math, Grade 6

Compare Absolute Values

Solve.

1. Jamie scored -5 points on her turn at a trivia game. In Veronica's turn, she scored more points than Jamie. Use absolute value to describe Veronica's score as a loss.

   In this situation, $|-5|$ represents a loss of

   _____ points. Veronica lost _____ than 5 points.

2. The low temperature on Friday was $-10°F$. The low temperature on Saturday was colder. Use absolute value to describe the temperature on Saturday as a temperature below zero.

   The temperature on Saturday was _____ than 10 degrees below zero.

3. The table shows changes in the savings accounts of five students. Which student had the greatest increase in money? By how much did the student's account increase?

   _____

Student	Account Change ($)
Brett	-12
Destiny	-36
Carissa	15
Rylan	10

Compare. Write $<$, $>$, or $=$.

4. $-16 \bigcirc |-16|$

5. $20 \bigcirc |20|$

6. $3 \bigcirc |-4|$

7. $|-12| \bigcirc |-11|$

8. $|25| \bigcirc |27|$

9. $|-9| \bigcirc |9|$

MIXED APPLICATIONS

10. On Wednesday, Miguel's bank account balance was $-\$55$. On Thursday, his balance was less than that. Use absolute value to describe Miguel's balance on Thursday as a debt.

    In this situation, $-\$55$ represents a debt of

    _____. On Thursday, Miguel had a

    debt of _____ than $55.

11. During a game, Naomi lost points. She lost fewer than 3 points. Use an integer to describe her possible score.

    _____

Variables and Expressions

Write an algebraic expression for each word expression.

1. 25 more than a number t _____

2. r fewer than 110.1 _____

3. 13 less than a number x _____

4. y less than 100 _____

5. the sum of 4.3 and a number d _____

6. q more than 67 _____

Write a word expression for each algebraic expression.

7. $43 + k$ _____

8. $15 - y$ _____

9. $v + 3.4$ _____

10. $a - 54$ _____

11. $t + 34$ _____

12. $x + 8.7$ _____

MIXED APPLICATIONS

13. The Pirates scored 10 more points than the Mavericks. Let p represent the number of points the Mavericks scored. Write an algebraic expression that represents the number of points the Pirates scored.

    _____

14. Gary is 15 years old. Let s represent Sandy's age. Write an algebraic expression that represents how many years older Sandy is than Gary.

    _____

15. A basketball team scores 83 points in their first game and 97 points in their second game. What was the total number of points scored in the two games?

    _____

16. In 1984 a tennis player earned $2,173,556 in prize money. Round that amount to the nearest hundred thousand dollars.

    _____

WRITER'S CORNER

17. Write a word problem similar to Exercise 13 that can be solved by using the expression $m + 5$.

    _____

    _____

The Language of Algebra

Write a word expression for each algebraic expression.

1. $x - 7$ _____

2. $u + 9$ _____

3. $6 + w$ _____

4. $m - 12$ _____

5. $5 - q$ _____

6. $6n$ _____

7. $15t$ _____

8. $\frac{c}{4}$ _____

9. $v + 8$ _____

10. $7p$ _____

Complete the table. Write an algebraic expression, an equation, or a word phrase.

	Word Expression or Sentence	Algebraic Expression or Equation
11.	t plus 10	
12.	y and six equals eight	
13.		$-7 + m$
14.	ten less than w is 15	
15.	t divided by five	
16.	12 is three times f	

MIXED APPLICATIONS

17. Tori was 15 years old in 2010. How old was she in 2000?

_____

18. Koko's pay increased by $0.50 an hour. What expression can show the increase in her pay?

_____

LOGICAL REASONING

19. Ronnie is thinking of a number. He says that he gets the same result when he multiplies his number by 2 as when he adds 5 to his number. What is his number?

_____

117

Writing Expressions with Variables

Write an algebraic expression for each verbal expression. Use the variable *n* when no variable is indicated.

1. *y* multiplied by *z* _____

2. the difference between *e* and *f* _____

3. the sum of *p* and *q* _____

4. the quotient of *b* and 7 _____

5. 2 more than *r* _____

6. *a* decreased by 6 _____

7. 12 divided by a number _____

8. the product of 3 and a number _____

9. 8 less than a number _____

10. a number increased by 1 _____

11. a number times 100 _____

12. a number subtracted from 20 _____

13. 32 decreased by *t* _____

14. 7 multiplied by a number _____

15. 28 separated into *g* equal parts _____

16. the difference between 25 and a number _____

Identifying Parts of Expressions

Identify the parts of each expression. Then write a word expression for the numerical or algebraic expression.

1. $(16 - 7) \div 3$

_____

_____

_____

_____

2. $20 + 5 \times 9$

_____

_____

_____

_____

3. $2e - f$

_____

_____

_____

_____

4. $8 + 6q + q$

_____

_____

_____

_____

Identify the terms of each expression. Then give the coefficient of each term.

5. $11r + 7s$

_____

_____

6. $6g - h$

_____

_____

MIXED APPLICATIONS

7. Adam bought granola bars at the store. The expression $6p + 5n$ gives the number of bars in p boxes of plain granola bars and n boxes of granola bars with nuts. What are the terms of the expression?

_____

8. In the sixth grade, each student will get 4 new books. There is one class of 15 students and one class of 20 students. The expression $4 \times (15 + 20)$ gives the total number of new books. Write a word expression for the numerical expression.

_____

Expressions: Addition and Subtraction

Evaluate each expression for $x = 5$.

1. $x + 2.7$ _____

2. $x + 12$ _____

3. $x - 3\frac{4}{7}$ _____

Evaluate each expression for $n = 15$.

4. $n - 6$ _____

5. $52 - n$ _____

6. $n - 15 + 15$ _____

Write the algebraic expression for each statement.

7. 19 less than a number, t

8. thirty-four increased by the sum of thirteen and a number, n

_____

Write each expression in words.

9. $t - 7$

10. $29 + n$

_____

11. $23 - r$

12. $c + (5 + 22)$

_____

MIXED APPLICATIONS

13. Danielle has n dollars in her wallet. She pays $5.19 for a book. What expression shows how much money she has left?

_____

14. Find all the numbers that are less than 200 and have the prime factors 3, 5, and 13.

_____

VISUAL THINKING

15. The number line is marked in whole numbers. Use the variable d to write expressions for points A and B.

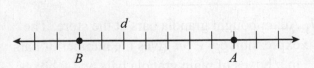

_____

Expressions: Multiplication and Division

Evaluate the expression $\frac{z}{8}$ for the values shown.

1. $z = 19.2$ **2.** $z = 92$ **3.** $z = 16.016$ **4.** $z = 5\frac{4}{9}$

_____   _____   _____   _____

Evaluate each expression. Let $m = 32$ and $n = 150$.

5. $\frac{m}{16}$ _____   **6.** $2n - 200$ _____   **7.** $\frac{3}{4}m - 12$ _____

Write an algebraic expression for each word expression.

8. the product of 14 and a number, x

9. a number, n, divided by 9

_____   _____

Write each expression in words.

10. $\frac{z}{11}$

11. $z + 11$

_____   _____

MIXED APPLICATIONS

12. The amount of cashews in a mixture of nuts is 3 times the amount of almonds. Let c represent the amount of cashews in the mixture. If there are $1\frac{1}{2}$ lb of almonds in the nut mixture, how many pounds of cashews are there?

_____

13. Josh is one-third as old as his mother. If Josh's mother is 45 years old, how old is Josh?

_____

SCIENCE CONNECTION

14. The formula for distance is $d = r \times t$, where d = distance, r = rate, and t = time. If a car travels for 15 seconds at 88 feet per second, how far will it have traveled?

_____

Name _____ Date _____

More Adding and Subtracting Expressions

Write an algebraic expression for each word expression.

1. $12 more than the cost of a CD player, c

2. the number of club members, m, increased by 5

_____

_____

3. 16 less than the number of sandwiches, s

4. the number of apples picked, a, minus 33

_____

_____

Write two word expressions for each algebraic expression.

5. $t - 7$ _____

_____

6. $r + 1.2$ _____

_____

Evaluate each expression for $b = 4$, $n = 1.5$, and $x = 10$.

7. $n + 13$ _____

8. $b - 2$ _____

9. $24 - x$ _____

10. $8.5 - n$ _____

11. $b + 21$ _____

12. $6^2 - n$ _____

13. $b + n$ _____

14. $x - b$ _____

MIXED APPLICATIONS

15. Jil paid $20 more for a car radio than she had expected. Write an expression that represents how much Jil paid. Let p represent the amount she had expected to pay.

16. Pete bought a hardbound book on sale at $3.25 off the regular price, r. Write an expression that represents the sale price of the book.

_____

_____

LOGICAL REASONING

17. If the value of $x - 10$ is 45, what is the value of $x - 15$?

_____

© Houghton Mifflin Harcourt Publishing Company

Evaluating Expressions

Evaluate the expression $x + 1.76$ for each value of x.

1. $x = 1.45$ **2.** $x = 8.9$ **3.** $x = 89.921$ **4.** $x = 36.4$ **5.** $x = 0.15$

_____ _____ _____ _____ _____

Evaluate each expression $122.43 - x$ for each value of x.

6. $x = 17.22$ **7.** $x = 25.13$ **8.** $x = 78.7$ **9.** $x = 23.778$ **10.** $x = 0.689$

_____ _____ _____ _____ _____

Evaluate each expression.

11. $z - 23$, for $z = 77$ _____   **12.** $a + 8.1$ for $a = 3.4$ _____

13. $68 + b$, for $b = 25$ _____   **14.** $35.9 - c$, for $c = 4.78$ _____

15. $46 - k$, for $k = 46$ _____   **16.** $84 - r$, for $r = 0$ _____

17. $(6 + w) + 13$, for $w = 2$ _____   **18.** $(y - 35) + 10$, for $y = 43$ _____

19. $(2.3 + 5.6) + v$, for $v = 4.7$ _____   **20.** $78 - (f + 11.1)$, for $f = 12.3$ _____

21. $m + (23.4 + 4.6)$, for $m = 10.98$ _____   **22.** $(b - 12.7) - 14.6$, for $b = 34$ _____

23. $7.05 + (p - 1.09)$, for $p = 5.1$ _____   **24.** $(t + 6.13) - 2.4$, for $t = 100$ _____

MIXED APPLICATIONS

25. Jeremy weighs 12 pounds more than he did a year ago. How much did he weigh a year ago if he now weights 146 pounds?

_____

26. Suki scored a 9.35 on the balance beam in a gymnastics meet. What was Kachina's score if she scored 0.585 more than Suki?

_____

NUMBER SENSE

27. Reverse the digits of 432 and subtract the smaller number from the larger number. Repeat this procedure five more times. What is the final difference?

_____

28. Use the procedure described in Exercise 27 using the number 781. How many times do you have to subtract to get the same result?

_____

More Multiplying and Dividing Expressions

Evaluate the expression 3.6*a* for each value of *a*.

1. *a* = 32 _____   **2.** *a* = 23 _____   **3.** *a* = 125 _____   **4.** *a* = 12.7 _____

Evaluate the expression $\frac{a}{8}$ for each value of *a*.

5. *a* = 64 _____   **6.** *a* = 208 _____   **7.** *a* = 1,700 _____   **8.** *a* = 118.4 _____

Evaluate each expression.

9. 24*b*, for *b* = 5

10. $\frac{t}{3}$, for *t* = 144

11. 54*c*, for *c* = 4

_____   _____   _____

12. $\frac{m}{12}$, for *m* = 672

13. 4.3*j*, for *j* = 1.2

14. $\frac{d}{3.8}$, for *d* = 23.94

_____   _____   _____

15. 4.6*r*, for *r* = 3.45

16. $\frac{y}{7}$, for *y* = 15.75

17. 5.67*n*, for *n* = 1.4

_____   _____   _____

18. $\frac{w}{1.5}$, for *w* = 10.35

19. 67*s*, for *s* = 34.9

20. $\frac{h}{7.4}$, for *h* = 26.27

_____   _____   _____

MIXED APPLICATIONS

For Exercises 21–22, write an algebraic expression. Then evaluate the expression.

21. Kris spent *d* dollars at school last week for lunches. If Kris attended school 5 days last week, how much did he spend on lunch each day? Evaluate the expression for *d* = $11.25.

22. Perry walks *s* miles each day. How many miles does Perry walk each week? Evaluate the expression for *s* = 5.

_____

_____

WRITER'S CORNER

23. Write a problem similar to Exercise 22 that can be solved by using the expression 4*m*.

_____

Variables and Expressions

Evaluate the expression $y - 10$ for each value of y.

1. $y = 14$ _____

2. $y = 48$ _____

3. $y = 12\frac{3}{8}$ _____

4. $y = -6$ _____

5. $y = -10$ _____

6. $y = 8$ _____

7. $y = 5$ _____

8. $y = -4$ _____

9. $y = 23.6$ _____

10. $y = -1$ _____

11. $y = 1$ _____

12. $y = 0$ _____

Evaluate the expression $t \div 4$ for each value of t.

13. $t = 12$ _____

14. $t = \frac{1}{4}$ _____

15. $t = 3\frac{1}{4}$ _____

16. $t = 64$ _____

17. $t = \frac{1}{2}$ _____

18. $t = 72$ _____

19. $t = 2\frac{8}{9}$ _____

20. $t = 100$ _____

21. $t = 17$ _____

22. $t = 25$ _____

23. $t = \frac{1}{8}$ _____

24. $t = 10$ _____

Evaluate the expression $9h$ for each value of h.

25. $h = 10$ _____

26. $h = 2\frac{1}{2}$ _____

27. $h = 6\frac{2}{3}$ _____

28. $h = 3.1$ _____

29. $h = 1.4$ _____

30. $h = 9.9$ _____

31. $h = 5.76$ _____

32. $h = 0.71$ _____

33. $h = 26$ _____

34. $h = 4.6$ _____

35. $h = 0.02$ _____

36. $h = \frac{1}{9}$ _____

MIXED APPLICATIONS

37. Geoffrey has 6 more books than Jorge. Let b equal the number of books Geoffrey has. Write an equation using 6 for the number of books Jorge has.

38. Jasmine walked 2 mi farther than Jennifer. Let m equal the number of miles Jennifer walked. Write an expression for the distance Jasmine walked. Then tell how far Jasmine walked if Jennifer walked 3 mi.

LOGICAL REASONING

39. Is $6 - r$ the same as $r - 6$? Explain.

125

Evaluating Expressions with Variables

Evaluate each expression if $a = 9$, $b = 3$, and $c = 7$.

1. $4a + 7$

2. $c(c + 3)$

3. $7b + 2b$

4. $(7 + 2)b$

_____

_____

_____

_____

5. $2bc$

6. $ab + ac$

7. $a(b + c)$

8. $ab + c$

_____

_____

_____

_____

9. $c(a - b)$

10. $ca - cb$

11. $ca - b$

12. $cb - a$

_____

_____

_____

_____

13. $\dfrac{a + b}{2}$

14. $\dfrac{2a + 2b}{4}$

15. $\dfrac{a}{b} + 9$

16. $\dfrac{a + 9}{b}$

_____

_____

_____

_____

Evaluate each expression if $x = 10$, $y = 25$, and $z = 20$.

17. $x + y$

18. $2y - 3x$

19. $3xy$

20. $3yx$

_____

_____

_____

_____

21. $z + 5x$

22. $y - 2x$

23. $(y - z)(z - x)$

24. $x(x + 2)$

_____

_____

_____

_____

25. $\dfrac{2}{3}(y - x)$

26. $\dfrac{2(y - x)}{3}$

27. $\dfrac{x}{2(y - z)}$

28. $\dfrac{x}{2}(y - z)$

_____

_____

_____

_____

Exploring Relations

Complete each table. Then write an expression using *x* to show the value of *y*.

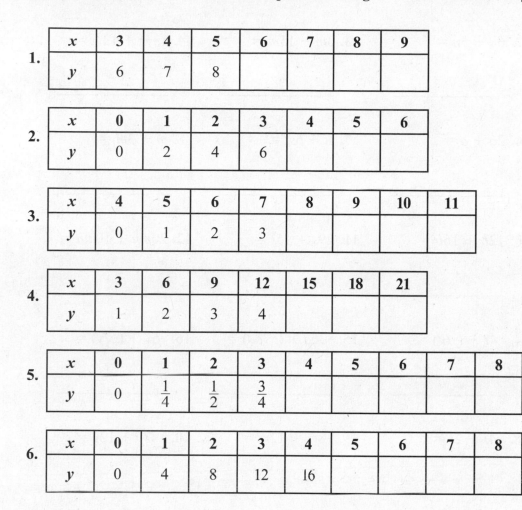

1.

x	3	4	5	6	7	8	9
y	6	7	8				

_____

2.

x	0	1	2	3	4	5	6
y	0	2	4	6			

_____

3.

x	4	5	6	7	8	9	10	11
y	0	1	2	3				

_____

4.

x	3	6	9	12	15	18	21
y	1	2	3	4			

_____

5.

x	0	1	2	3	4	5	6	7	8
y	0	$\frac{1}{4}$	$\frac{1}{2}$	$\frac{3}{4}$					

_____

6.

x	0	1	2	3	4	5	6	7	8
y	0	4	8	12	16				

_____

7. In Exercise 3, what expression can you write, using *y*, to show the value of *x*?

_____

8. In Exercise 4, what expression can you write, using *y*, to show the value of *x*?

_____

WRITER'S CORNER

9. Decide on a relation between *x* and *y*. Then set up a table showing the relation. Ask a friend or family member to write the expression that shows the value of *y*.

x								
y								

127

Adding Like Terms

Find each sum.

1. $2y + 4y =$

2. $6n + 5n =$

3. $3m + 15m =$

4. $13yz + 12yz =$

_____   _____   _____   _____

5. $5x + x =$

6. $2a + a =$

7. $st + 6st =$

8. $m + 3m =$

_____   _____   _____   _____

9. $28y + 52y =$

10. $12b + 16b =$

11. $29s + 15s =$

12. $20mn + 10mn =$

_____   _____   _____   _____

13. $3x + (-2x) =$

14. $-4t + (-6t) =$

15. $-3cd + (-7cd) =$

16. $-5v + (-7v) =$

_____   _____   _____   _____

17. $-2ab + 7ab =$

18. $-4t + 2t =$

19. $-8rs + 12rs =$

20. $-43y + 12y =$

_____   _____   _____   _____

21. $\frac{1}{2}a + \frac{1}{2}a =$

22. $\frac{1}{3}n + \frac{1}{3}n =$

23. $\frac{13}{4}x + \frac{1}{4}x =$

24. $d + \frac{1}{2}d =$

_____   _____   _____   _____

25. $0.5b + 1.3b =$

26. $3.2y + 0.8y =$

27. $0.8k + 0.2k =$

28. $0.05t + 0.07t =$

_____   _____   _____   _____

29. $3a + 2a + 4a =$

30. $5xy + xy + 8xy =$

31. $6m + 9m + 3m =$

32. $7h + h + 2h =$

_____   _____   _____   _____

Subtracting Like Terms

Find each difference.

1. $7y - 5y =$

2. $8a - 7a =$

3. $14rt - 7rt =$

4. $20w - 14w =$

5. $3h - 5h =$

6. $8yz - 11yz =$

7. $2f - 9f =$

8. $8mn - 17mn =$

9. $-2x - 7x =$

10. $-4g - 8g =$

11. $-5z - 9z =$

12. $-24b - 35b =$

13. $6n - n =$

14. $4p - p =$

15. $-3k - k =$

16. $-5r - 5r =$

17. $7t - 5t =$

18. $m - 7m =$

19. $a - 12a =$

20. $xy - 28xy =$

21. $-5ab - (-9ab) =$

22. $-4k - (-8k) =$

23. $-7t - (-6t) =$

24. $-8x - (-3x) =$

25. $\frac{3}{4}t - \frac{1}{4}t =$

26. $\frac{4}{5}x - \frac{3}{5}x =$

27. $\frac{2}{3}h - \frac{1}{3}h =$

28. $\frac{3}{2}b - \frac{1}{2}b =$

29. $0.3n - 0.12n =$

30. $3.2a - 2.7a =$

31. $5.4k - 4.7k =$

32. $6st - 4.2st =$

Adding and Subtracting Like Terms

Find each sum or difference.

1. $-3xy - 2xy =$

_____

2. $-7mn + (14mn) =$

_____

3. $-13k - (-4k) =$

_____

4. $0.7c - 0.3c =$

_____

5. $15pq + (-25pq) =$

_____

6. $h - 3h =$

_____

7. $-9v - (-8v) =$

_____

8. $15ab + ab + 6ab =$

_____

9. $2.8n - 3.5n =$

_____

10. $\frac{3}{5}b + \frac{2}{5}b =$

_____

11. $18pr - (4pr) =$

_____

12. $-9wx - 9wx =$

_____

13. $25z - 8z + (-3z) =$

_____

14. $-5lm - -9lm =$

_____

15. $10u + (-15u) =$

_____

16. $7s + (2s) - (19s) =$

_____

17. $7z + -2z =$

_____

18. $-5u - 1.9u =$

_____

19. $-6rp + (-3rp) =$

_____

20. $-7b - (-29b) =$

_____

21. $-26ty + (-4ty) =$

_____

22. $-21c + 6c =$

_____

23. $2.9c + (-3c) =$

_____

24. $-5fg + (-17fg) =$

_____

25. $9r - (-3r) + 12r =$

_____

26. $-79h + (-9h) =$

_____

27. $-16ds + (-9ds) =$

_____

28. $-5j + j + (-14j) =$

_____

29. $-\frac{4}{7}en - \frac{3}{7}en =$

_____

30. $3.01i - 1.52i =$

_____

31. $-8w - 6w + 3w =$

_____

32. $-20x - 9x =$

_____

33. $7kl - (-8kl) + kl =$

_____

34. $-13dh + (-10dh) =$

_____

35. $-1.3s + 3s - 4s =$

_____

36. $-3q + 7q - 4q =$

_____

Simplifying Expressions

Simplify each expression.

1. $5a + 4a - 2a =$ _____

2. $8g + 3g - 7g =$ _____

3. $4x - 12x + 7x =$ _____

4. $6y - 4y + y =$ _____

5. $3m - 5m + 4m =$ _____

6. $12b - 8b - 4b =$ _____

7. $9a - 6a + 3b =$ _____

8. $7t + 4s + 5t =$ _____

9. $6ab - 3ac - 8ac =$ _____

10. $5r - 7r + 8m =$ _____

11. $11 - 4k - 9k =$ _____

12. $5x - 7 + 9 =$ _____

13. $16xy - 18 + 7xy =$ _____

14. $4f - 9f - 3f + 10 =$ _____

15. $-8rs + 9rs + st =$ _____

16. $-4g - 5 - 3g + 8 =$ _____

17. $e + ef + 5ef =$ _____

18. $3x - 7x - 9x =$ _____

19. $19 + 15bc - 3bc + 2 =$ _____

20. $31p - 54p - 82p =$ _____

21. $-36 + 74r - 53 + r =$ _____

Generate Equivalent Expressions

Use properties of operations and combining like terms to write an expression equivalent to each of these expressions.

1. $7h - 3h$

2. $5x + 7 + 2x$

3. $16 + 13p - 9p$

_____

_____

_____

4. $y^2 + 13y - 8y$

5. $5(2h + 3) + 3h$

6. $12 + 18n + 7 - 14n$

_____

_____

_____

Use the Distributive Property to write equivalent expressions.

7. $2(9 + 5k)$

8. $5(3m + 2)$

9. $6(g + h)$

_____

_____

_____

10. $4d + 8$

11. $21p + 35q$

12. $18x + 9y$

_____

_____

_____

MIXED APPLICATIONS

13. The expression $15n + 12n + 100$ represents the total cost in dollars for skis, boots, and a lesson for n skiers. Simplify the expression $15n + 12n + 100$. Then find the total cost for 8 skiers.

14. Casey has n nickels. Megan has 4 times as many nickels as Casey has. Write an expression for the total number of nickels Casey and Megan have. Then simplify the expression.

_____

_____

132

Identifying Equivalent Expressions

Use properties of operations to determine whether the expressions are equivalent.

1. $2s + 13 + 15s$ and $17s + 13$

_____

2. $5 \times 7h$ and $35h$

_____

3. $10 + 8v - 3v$ and $18 - 3v$

_____

4. $(9w \div 0) - 12$ and $9w - 12$

_____

5. $11(p + q)$ and $11p + (7q + 4q)$

_____

6. $6(4b + 3d)$ and $24b + 3d$

_____

7. $14m + 9 - 6m$ and $8m + 9$

_____

8. $(y \times 1) + 2$ and $y + 2$

_____

9. $4 + 5(6t + 1)$ and $9 + 30t$

_____

10. $9x + 0 + 10x$ and $19x + 1$

_____

11. $12c - 3c$ and $3(4c - 1)$

_____

12. $6a \times 4$ and $24a$

_____

MIXED APPLICATIONS

13. Rachel needs to write 3 book reports with b pages and 3 science reports with s pages during the school year. Write an algebraic expression for the total number of pages Rachel will need to write.

_____

14. Rachel's friend Yassi has to write $3(b + s)$ pages for reports. Use properties of operations to determine whether this expression is equivalent to the expression for the number of pages Rachel has to write.

_____

Addition Equations

Solve each equation. Check your solutions.

1. $n + 8 = 13$

_____

2. $b + 17 = 62$

_____

3. $x + \dfrac{5}{6} = 7\dfrac{1}{6}$

_____

4. $y + \dfrac{1}{7} = \dfrac{5}{8}$

_____

5. $14 + y = 69$

_____

6. $c + 3.6 = 4.9$

_____

Write and solve an equation for each statement. Use the variable *n*.

7. A number increased by 19 is 221.

_____

8. A number increased by $1\dfrac{2}{3}$ is 8.

_____

9. The sum of a number and $6\dfrac{1}{5}$ is $8\dfrac{2}{3}$.

_____

10. 5.4 more than a number is 23.1.

_____

11. A number increased by the sum of 3 and 2.6 is 9.

_____

12. 29 more than a number is 113.

_____

MIXED APPLICATIONS

13. Lita jogged $2\dfrac{2}{3}$ miles more on Wednesday than on Tuesday. She jogged $4\dfrac{1}{2}$ miles on Wednesday. Write and solve an equation to find how many miles she jogged on Tuesday.

_____

14. A wildlife refuge has about 10^5 elk. Are there more than or fewer than 1 million elk in the refuge?

_____

MIXED REVIEW

Find each product or quotient.

15. $9\dfrac{3}{5} \div 3\dfrac{1}{5}$ _____

16. $4.8 \div 12$ _____

17. $32\dfrac{1}{2} \times 2\dfrac{2}{13}$ _____

Subtraction Equations

Solve each equation. Check your solutions.

1. $a - 65 = 7$ **2.** $x - 58 = 16$ **3.** $x - 4\frac{3}{8} = 6$

_____   _____   _____

4. $c - 42 = 67$ **5.** $y - 4.8 = 9.2$ **6.** $b - 4\frac{1}{4} = 2\frac{2}{3}$

_____   _____   _____

Use addition or subtraction to solve each equation. Check your solutions.

7. $a - 2\frac{2}{9} = 1\frac{1}{2}$ **8.** $c - 6.005 = 2.5$ **9.** $b + 55 = 83$

_____   _____   _____

MIXED APPLICATIONS

Write an equation for each problem. Use the variable _m_.

10. Five students are absent from math class today. If there are 22 students in math class today, how many students would there be if none were absent?

_____

11. Juan pays $22.05 more than Kim each month for his health club membership. Juan pays $58.95 each month. How much does Kim pay each month?

_____

VISUAL THINKING

12. Carl had part of a pizza. He gave $\frac{1}{6}$ of a pizza to Susan. He still had the amount shown. What part of a pizza did Carl have at first? Use the variable _p_.

_____

Solve the equation for _p_.

_____

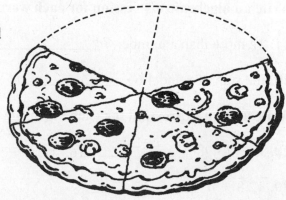

Exploring Addition and Subtraction Equations

Tell how to solve each equation.

1. $x + 2 = 5$

_____

2. $y - 9 = 12$

_____

3. $m + 24 = 32$

_____

4. $c + 10 = 15$

_____

5. $t + 13 = 25$

_____

6. $b - 26 = 14$

_____

7. $1.7 + a = 5.67$

_____

8. $z + 7.6 = 9.1$

_____

9. $k - 3.34 = 1.2$

_____

10. $c - 8.5 = 4.6$

_____

11. $43.8 + r = 36.9$

_____

12. $p + 23.4 = 56.8$

_____

Use inverse operations to solve each equation.

13. $x + 12 = 21$ _____

14. $8 + n = 14$ _____

15. $t - 8 = 13$ _____

16. $6 + t = 19$ _____

17. $m - 17 = 9$ _____

18. $r - 1.2 = 2.3$ _____

MIXED REVIEW

Find each sum or difference.

19.	**20.**	**21.**	**22.**	**23.**
9,089	78,098	16,903	345,897	80,443
+ 2,567	− 65,739	+ 24,456	− 237,764	− 59,965

Write an algebraic expression for each word expression.

24. 12 more than a number, t _____

25. 9 fewer than a number, r _____

26. the sum of x and 4.6 _____

27. u less than 9.7 _____

Write a word expression for each algebraic expression.

28. $w - 13.98$ _____

29. $c + 235$ _____

30. $12.8 + d$ _____

31. $7.3 - s$ _____

Multiplication Equations

Solve each equation. Check your solutions.

1. $6n = 42$

_____

2. $3y = 192$

_____

3. $8x = 72$

_____

4. $4y = 28$

_____

5. $7n = 112$

_____

6. $8x = 272$

_____

7. $7n = 49$

_____

8. $33y = 66$

_____

9. $6b = 96$

_____

10. $5n = 280$

_____

11. $6n = 72$

_____

12. $13r = 169$

_____

13. $5.4k = 21.6$

_____

14. $4.5a = 9.0$

_____

15. $4.8b = 36$

_____

MIXED APPLICATIONS

Write an equation for each problem using the variable n. Then solve and check each equation.

16. Akio has 84 baseball cards. This is 19 fewer cards than Mike has. How many baseball cards does Mike have?

_____

17. Janelle can ride her bike 3 times as fast as Michelle can jog. If Janelle rides her bike at a rate of 12 miles per hour, how fast can Michelle jog?

_____

NUMBER SENSE

Mentally solve each equation.

18. $5 + r = 6 - r$

_____

19. $z - 16 = -16$

_____

20. $7n - 7 = 0$

_____

Division Equations

Solve each equation. Check your solutions.

1. $\dfrac{x}{4} = 9$

_____

2. $\dfrac{a}{5} = 7$

_____

3. $\dfrac{n}{3} = 29$

_____

4. $\dfrac{n}{3} = 10$

_____

5. $\dfrac{x}{5} = 24$

_____

6. $\dfrac{b}{9} = 15$

_____

7. $\dfrac{n}{7} = 17$

_____

8. $\dfrac{x}{3} = 8$

_____

9. $\dfrac{y}{5} = 33$

_____

10. $\dfrac{e}{36} = 5$

_____

11. $\dfrac{a}{25} = 4$

_____

12. $\dfrac{b}{16} = 7$

_____

MIXED APPLICATIONS

Write an equation for each exercise using the variable *n*. Then solve and check each one.

13. If a number, *n*, divided by 8 equals 2.5, what is *n*?

_____

14. The sum of a number, *n*, and 6.05 is 12.4. What is *n*?

_____

15. Stacy is one-fourth as old as her mother. If Stacy's mother is 36, how old is Stacy?

_____

16. One-third of a painting job takes 24 hours. How long will it take to complete the entire job?

_____

NUMBER SENSE

Estimate the solution for each equation.

17. $6b = 110$

_____

18. $4n = 159$

_____

19. $\dfrac{14}{x} = 5$

_____

Name _____ Date _____

Exploring Multiplication and Division Equations

Complete.

By using a balance scale, you can solve the equation $4d = 40$ to find that $d = 10$.

1. What is the inverse of multiplication? _____

2. What operation should you use to solve the
   equation $4d = 40$ to find the value of d? _____

Suppose you were asked to solve the equation $\frac{d}{4} = 10$.

3. What is the inverse of division? _____

4. What operation would you use to solve the equation? _____

5. How would you solve the equation $\frac{d}{4} = 10$ to find
   the value of d? _____

Tell how to solve each equation.

6. $2x = 10$ _____   7. $\frac{c}{3} = 15$ _____   8. $10m = 20$ _____

9. $\frac{s}{5} = 13$ _____   10. $8f = 122$ _____

11. $5y = 16$ _____   12. $15z = 180$ _____

13. $\frac{u}{8} = 18$ _____   14. $\frac{a}{14} = 100$ _____

15. $35t = 525$ _____   16. $\frac{d}{3} = 135$ _____

17. $\frac{y}{13} = 7$ _____   18. $12f = 360$ _____

19. $63k = 315$ _____   20. $\frac{p}{116} = 1$ _____

Use the inverse operation to solve each equation.

21. $5t = 60$ _____   22. $3n = 39$ _____   23. $\frac{d}{4} = 10$ _____

24. $18x = 252$ _____   25. $\frac{w}{5} = 21$ _____   26. $9h = 459$ _____

139

Equations with Whole Numbers and Fractions

Tell the inverse of the operation for each equation.

1. $x - 5 = 7$ _____

2. $r + 4 = 8$ _____

3. $\frac{4}{5} + w = 5$ _____

4. $u - \frac{1}{2} = 13$ _____

5. $m - 7 = 1\frac{2}{5}$ _____

6. $19 = r + 4$ _____

Use inverse operations to solve each equation.

7. $x + 202 = 300$ _____

8. $y - 413 = 521$ _____

9. $m + 147 = 205$ _____

10. $x + \frac{1}{5} = \frac{4}{5}$ _____

11. $t - \frac{3}{4} = 1$ _____

12. $q + 2\frac{1}{4} = 7$ _____

13. $x + \frac{2}{7} = \frac{9}{14}$ _____

14. $c - \frac{2}{3} = \frac{1}{6}$ _____

15. $n + 3\frac{3}{4} = 19$ _____

16. $z + 4 = 6\frac{1}{8}$ _____

17. $d - \frac{1}{3} = \frac{5}{6}$ _____

18. $m + \frac{7}{11} = 1$ _____

19. $r + 18,454 = 76,000$ _____

20. $s - 46,889 = 90,000$ _____

MIXED APPLICATIONS

21. Jan flew the first 246 mi of her trip and then drove the rest of the way. Let d equal the number of miles she drove. Write an expression for the number of miles in Jan's trip.

_____

22. A peach tree produced 168 peaches. Another peach tree produced 39 fewer peaches. How many peaches did the other tree produce?

_____

MIXED REVIEW

Write the greatest common factor (GCF) for each pair of numbers.

23. 6, 12 _____

24. 8, 14 _____

25. 24, 36 _____

26. 7, 21 _____

Write the prime factorization in exponent form for each number.

27. 16 _____

28. 35 _____

29. 50 _____

30. 63 _____

Are the ratios equivalent? Write *yes* or *no*.

31. $\frac{7}{10}; \frac{6}{9}$ _____

32. $\frac{1}{5}; \frac{5}{25}$ _____

33. $\frac{8}{15}; \frac{24}{45}$ _____

34. $\frac{10}{14}; \frac{5}{6}$ _____

Equations with Integers

Tell what integers to add or subtract to solve each equation.

1. $m = 11 + {-8}$ _____

2. $s = {-9} + 4$ _____

3. $r - 6 = 3$ _____

4. $n - {-3} = 7$ _____

5. $t + {-16} = 14$ _____

6. $c - 7 = {-6}$ _____

7. $b - {-4} = 3$ _____

8. $z + 35 = 24$ _____

9. $q - 8 = 5$ _____

10. $n + {-4} = {-7}$ _____

Solve each equation.

11. $s = 15 + {-7}$ _____

12. $d = 15 - {-8}$ _____

13. $w = {-4} - {-2}$ _____

14. $t + {-9} = {-10}$ _____

15. $y - 6 = {-8}$ _____

16. $n + {-10} = 30$ _____

17. $h - 14 = 3$ _____

18. $a + 6 = 2$ _____

19. $w + {-5} = {-15}$ _____

20. $f - {-12} = 10$ _____

21. $u + 6 = {-9}$ _____

22. $z - 2 = {-9}$ _____

23. $z + {-8} = {-1}$ _____

24. $m = 3 - {-7}$ _____

25. $t + 13 = 3$ _____

26. If x is 8, what is $x + 14$? _____

27. If t is 14, what is $25 - t$? _____

28. If r is -6, what is $r + 3$? _____

29. If a is -8, what is $13 - a$? _____

MIXED APPLICATIONS

30. Suzanne wrote a check for $25. She now has $560 in her account. How much was in her account before she wrote the check?

_____

31. The temperature at 7:00 A.M. was -10°C. The temperature at noon was -15°C. What was the change in temperature from 7:00 A.M. to noon?

_____

NUMBER SENSE

Write the next two numbers in each pattern.

32. -8, -6, -7, -5, -6, -4, _____, _____

33. 3, 1, 5, 3, 7, 5, 9, _____, _____

Name _____   Date _____

Solutions of Equations

For each equation, determine whether the given value of the variable is a solution of the equation.

1. $x - 7 = 15; x = 8$

_____ $- 7 \overset{?}{=} 15$

_____ ◯ 15

_____

2. $c + 11 = 20; c = 9$

_____

3. $7n = 7; n = 0$

_____

4. $\frac{1}{3}h = 6; h = 2$

_____

5. $a - 1 = 70; a = 71$

_____

6. $\frac{7}{8} + j = 1; j = \frac{1}{8}$

_____

7. $16.1 + d = 22; d = 6.1$

_____

8. $9 = \frac{3}{4}e; e = 12$

_____

9. $15.5 - y = 7.9; y = 8.4$

_____

MIXED APPLICATIONS

10. Terrance needs to score 25 points to win a game. He has already scored 18 points. The equation $18 + p = 25$ gives the number of points, p, that Terrance still needs to score. Determine whether $p = 7$ or $p = 13$ is a solution of the equation, and tell what the solution means.

_____

_____

_____

11. Madeline has used 50 sheets of a roll of paper towels, which is $\frac{5}{8}$ of the entire roll. The equation $\frac{5}{8}s = 50$ can be used to find the number of sheets, s, in a full roll. Determine whether $s = 32$ or $s = 80$ is a solution of the equation, and tell what the solution means.

_____

_____

_____

Independent and Dependent Variables

Identify the independent and dependent variables. Then write an equation to represent the relationship between them.

1. Sandra has a coupon to save $3 off her next purchase at a restaurant. The cost of her meal, *c*, will be the price of the food, *p*, that she orders, minus $3.

   The cost of her meal depends on the price of her food.

   dependent variable: _____

   independent variable: _____

   equation: _____ = _____

2. An online clothing store charges $6 for shipping, no matter the price of the items. The total cost, *c*, in dollars is the price of the items ordered, *p*, plus $6 for shipping.

   dependent variable: _____

   independent variable: _____

   equation: _____ = _____

3. Melinda is making necklaces. She uses 12 beads for each necklace. The total number of beads, *b*, depends on the number of necklaces, *n*.

   dependent variable: _____

   independent variable: _____

   equation: _____ = _____

4. Tanner is 2 years younger than his brother. Tanner's age, *t*, in years is 2 less than his brother's age, *h*

   dependent variable: _____

   independent variable: _____

   equation: _____ = _____

5. Byron is playing a game. He earns 10 points for each question he answers correctly. His total score, *s*, equals the number of correct answers, *a*, times 10.

   dependent variable: _____

   independent variable: _____

   equation: _____ = _____

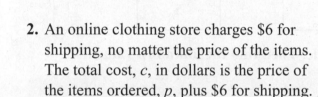

MIXED APPLICATIONS

6. Maria earns $45 for every lawn that she mows. Her earnings, *e*, in dollars depend on the number of lawns, *n*, that she mows. Write an equation that represents this situation.

   _____

7. Martin sells cars. He earns $100 per day, plus any commission on his sales. His daily salary, *s*, in dollars depends on the amount of commission, *c*. Write an equation to represent his daily salary.

   _____

143

Equations and Tables

Use the equation to complete each table.

1. $y = 6x$

Input	Output
x	y
2	
5	
8	

2. $y = x - 7$

Input	Output
x	y
10	
15	
20	

3. $y = 3x + 4$

Input	Output
x	y
3	
4	
5	

Write an equation for the relationship shown in each table. Then find the unknown value in each table.

4.

x	2	3	4	5
y	16	?	32	40

_____

5.

x	18	20	22	24
y	9	10	?	12

_____

6.

x	8	10	12	14
y	13	15	17	?

_____

7.

x	14	17	20	23
y	5	?	11	14

_____

MIXED APPLICATIONS

8. Tickets to a play cost $11 each. There is also a service charge of $4 per order. Write an equation for the relationship that gives the total cost, y, in dollars for an order of x tickets.

_____

9. Write an equation for the relationship shown in the table. Then use the equation to find the estimated number of shrimp in a 5-pound bag.

Weight of bag (pounds), x	1	2	3	4
Estimated number of shrimp, y	24	48	72	96

_____

Equations and Graphs

Complete the chart of orderd pairs
and graph the equation.

Graph the equation.

1. $y = x - 3$

x	y
5	2
6	
7	
8	

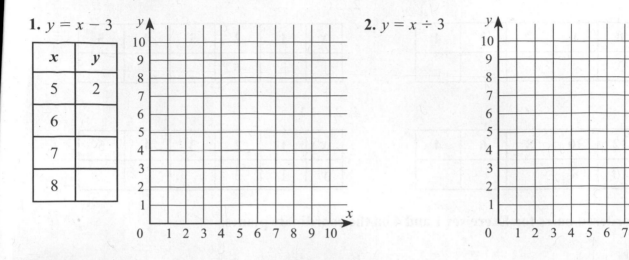

2. $y = x \div 3$

Write an equation for the relationship shown by the graph.

3.

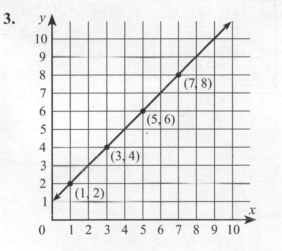

(7, 8)
(5, 6)
(3, 4)
(1, 2)

_____

4.

(2, 8)
(1.5, 6)
(1, 4)

_____

MIXED APPLICATIONS

5. Dee is driving at an average speed of 50 miles per hour. Write an equation for the relationship that gives the distance, y, in miles that Dee drives in x hours.

_____

6. Graph the relationship from Exercise 5.

_____

Dee's Distance

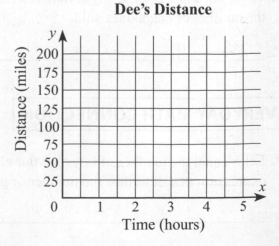

146

Graphing Relations

Use the expression to help you complete each table.

1. $x + 3$

x	0	1	2	3	4
y	3	4			

2. $3x$

x	1	2	3	4	5
y	3	6			

3. $x - 2$

x	12	10	8	6	4
y	10	8			

4. $2x - 1$

x	1	2	3	4	5
y	1	3			

Graph the ordered pairs for Exercises 1 and 4 on the coordinate planes.

5.

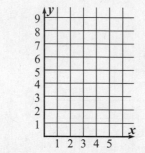

6.

MIXED APPLICATIONS

Use the table for Exercises 7–8.

Students (s)	1	2	3	4	5
Magazines sold (m)	6	11	16	21	26

7. Write the expression, using s, that describes the number of magazines sold.

_____

8. If the pattern continues, how many magazines will 10 students sell?

_____

EVERYDAY MATH CONNECTION

9. Let b equal the number of boys in your class. Write an expression that describes the number of girls in your class.

_____

145

Write Inequalities

Write an inequality for each word sentence. Tell what the variable represents and what kind of number the answer will be.

1. The width, *w*, is greater than 4 centimeters.

   _____

   _____

2. The score, *s*, in a basketball game is greater than or equal to 10 points.

   _____

3. The mass, *m*, is less than 5 kilograms.

   _____

   _____

4. The height, *h*, is greater than 2.5 meters.

   _____

5. The temperature, *t*, is less than or equal to $-3°$.

   _____

   _____

Write a word sentence for each inequality.

6. $k < -7$

   _____

7. $z \geq 14$

   _____

8. $m \leq 2\frac{3}{5}$

   _____

9. $f > 0.24$

   _____

MIXED APPLICATIONS

10. Tabby's mom says that she must read for at least 30 minutes each night. If *m* represents the number of minutes reading, what inequality can represent this situation?

    _____

11. Phillip has a $25 gift card to his favorite restaurant. He wants to use the gift card to buy lunch. If *c* represents the cost of his lunch, what inequality can describe all of the possible amounts of money, in dollars, that Phillip can spend on lunch?

    _____

Inequalities

Tell whether ⁻3 is a solution of each inequality. Write *yes* or *no*.

1. $y > 0$ _____

2. $x < ⁻1$ _____

3. $c + 1 > 5$ _____

Tell whether 2 is a solution of each inequality. Write *yes* or *no*.

4. $x - 1 < 0$ _____

5. $y + 2 > ⁻1$ _____

6. $d - 2 > 0$ _____

7. Which number line shows solutions of $x < 1$? Circle **a**, **b**, or **c**.

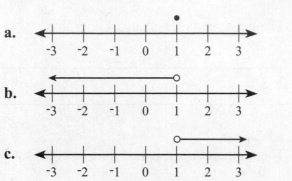

8. Which number line shows solutions of $y > ⁻2$? Circle **a**, **b**, or **c**.

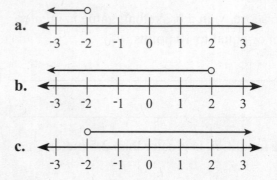

On the number line, show the solutions of each inequality.

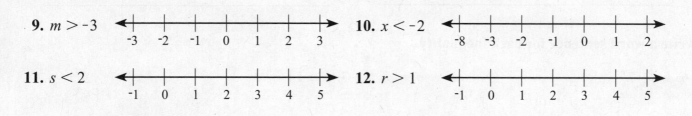

9. $m > ⁻3$

10. $x < ⁻2$

11. $s < 2$

12. $r > 1$

MIXED APPLICATIONS

Write an equation or inequality.

13. The number of books in Sandra's collection is more than 15.

_____

14. There were 100 people at the picnic, a number of adults and 25 children.

_____

NUMBER SENSE

15. Write two integers that are solutions to both $x > ⁻3$ and $x < 0$.

_____

Solutions of Inequalities

Determine whether the given value of the variable for each inequality is a solution of the inequality.

1. $s \geq -1; s = 1$ **2.** $p < 0; p = 4$ **3.** $y \leq -3; y = -1$

_____   _____   _____

4. $u > 2\frac{1}{2}; u = 0$ **5.** $q \geq 0.6; q = 0.23$ **6.** $b < 2\frac{3}{4}; b = \frac{2}{3}$

_____   _____   _____

7. $j \leq -5.7; j = -6$ **8.** $a > -8; a = -7.5$ **9.** $w \geq 4.5; w = 4.45$

_____   _____   _____

Give two solutions of each inequality.

10. $k < 2$ **11.** $z \geq -3$ **12.** $f \leq -5$

_____   _____   _____

MIXED APPLICATIONS

13. The inequality $s \geq 92$ represents the score, s, that Jared must earn on his next test to get an A on his report card. Give two possible scores that Jared could earn to get the A.

14. The inequality $m \leq \$20$ represents the amount of money that Sheila is allowed to spend on a new hat. Give two possible money amounts that Sheila could spend on the hat.

_____   _____

Answer Key

Page 1

1–5. Number sentences will vary.
6. 3; Associative Property
7. 5; Commutative Property
8. 2; Distributive Property
9. 6; Associative Property
10. 144
11. 0
12. 160
13. 720
14. 92
15. 75
16. $(3 \times 12) \times 2 = (3 \times 2) \times 12$; 72 pencils
17. $(6 \times 38) \times 3 = (6 \times 3) \times 38$; 684 mugs
18. 0
19. 82,462

Page 2

1. yes, no, yes, no, yes
2. no, yes, no, yes no
3. yes, yes, no, no, no
4. yes, yes, no, yes, no
5. no, no, no, no, no
6. yes, yes, yes, no, yes
7. no, yes, no, no, no
8. yes, yes, no, no, no
9. yes, yes, no, no, no
10. no, yes, yes, no, no
11. yes, yes, yes, yes, yes
12. a
13. b
14. Answers will vary.

Page 3

1. a
2. b
3. b
4. c
5. a
6–24. Estimates may vary. Possible estimates are given.
6. 150; 160
7. 190; 200
8. 600; 420
9. 500; 400
10. 300; 200
11. 50; 40
12. 900; 800
13. 20; 20

14. 18; 20
15. 70; 40
16. 1,250; 1,500
17. 210; 200
18. 15; 15
19. 70; 60
20. 160; 160
21. 400; 300
22. 700; 600
23. 9; 7
24. 70; 40
25. about 6 mi per min
26. about 30 pans
27. Answers will vary. Exercises 25 and 26 are examples

Page 4

1–15. Estimates may vary. One possible estimate is given.
1. 10
2. 50
3. 50
4. 100
5. 3,000
6. 80
7. 340
8. 1500
9. 20
10. 200
11. 120
12. 14,000
13. 1,500
14. 1,500
15. 4,000
16. 98
17. 654
18. 1,256
19. 6,369 r3
20. 15,655 r3
21. 945 r7
22. 3,057
23. 3,518 r6
24. 6,606 r2
25. 523 magazines
26. 144 chickens
27. yes; $36 \times 4 = 144$

Page 5

1–8. Answers will vary. One possible estimate is given.
1. 5
2. 6
3. 80
4. 100
5. 5
6. 500
7. 70
8. 900
9. 7 r17
10. 4 r9
11. 8 r1
12. 8 r15
13. 48 r68
14. 19 r97
15. 389 r4
16. 62 r20
17. 48 r12
18. 73 r1
19. 1,316 r26
20. 133 r 13
21. 96
22. 9,506
23. 12
24. 1,632
25. 23
26. 63
27. 1,292
28. 9
29. 6 bags
30. 2,050 pennies

Page 6

1–11. Estimates may vary. One possible estimate is given.
1. 400
2. 500
3. 4,000; 4,737
4. 900
5. 2,000; 2,314
6. 900
7. 4,000; 4,850 r6
8. 17,000; 17,551 r1
9. 600; 591 r2
10. 5,000; 4,866 r4
11. 7,000; 7,046 r5
12. $9,100
13. 7,039 coins
14. 5; Associative Property
15. 3; Distributive Property

150

Page 7

1. 201
2. 31
3. 91
4. 1,040
5. 600
6. 701
7. 74
8. 1,031 r21
9. 1,310 r21
10. 92
11. 1,201
12. 700 r10
13. 80 dolls
14. $500
15. >
16. >
17. <
18. <

Page 8

1. 604
2. 5
3. 482
4. 204
5. 5,616
6. 304
7. 400 r6
8. 320
9. 1,600
10. 2,070 r1
11. 302 r3
12. 204 r4
13. 350 r2
14. 90 r7
15. 720 stamps
16. 6 erasers
17. 2, 5, 10
18. 5
19. 2, 3
20. 3, 5, 9
21. b
22. b
23. 92
24. 312
25. 17
26. 12 r19

Page 9

1. 21.376
2. 24.843
3. 56.917
4. 351.659
5. 5.8
6. 42.62
7. 10.026
8. $60.13
9. 72.498
10. 13.156
11. 22.695
12. 63.469
13. 47.9694
14. 30.403
15. 663.63
16. $86.35
17. 3,770.1
18. 4.876 cm
19. 34.95 in.
20. 176,808 more cars
21. Vermont; 13,000
22. The decimal point is in a different place; no; the digits are the same, but they are in different places.

Page 10

1. 4.62
2. 11.47
3. 28.759
4. 5.85
5. 26.72
6. 165.89
7. 89.091
8. 0.179
9. 0.642
10. 3.649
11. 9.93
12. 14.781
13. 13.726
14. 1.326
15. 0.205
16. 59.02
17. 91.568
18. 8.36
19. 17.665
20. 3.31
21. 83.035
22. 69.25
23. 560.63
24. 57.0259
25. 36.85 sec
26. 1.15 yd
27. 3,100 mi
28. about 40 mph faster
29. The digits are the same; $106 - 89$ has the greater difference.

Page 11

1. 2
2. 3
3. 20
4. 510
5. 8.426
6. 2.949
7. 9.679
8. 424.093
9. 36.091
10. 559
11. 0.999
12. 299.012
13. 146.445 gallons of gas
14. A-One Gas; $0.06 per gallon
15. 0.006 iron, 0.06 magnesium, 0.165 sodium, 0.31 chlorine, 0.33 potassium, 0.36 sulfur, 1.8 phosphorous, 3 calcium, 4.5 nitrogen, 15 hydrogen, 27 carbon, 97.5 oxygen

Page 12

1. 23.12
2. 11.776
3. 51.5812
4. 4.508
5. 0.7372
6. 1.8805
7. 113.685
8. 324.3
9. 3.4744
10. 18,322.2
11. 23.12
12. 24.836
13. 1,596.7
14. $174.07
15. 2.872
16. 1,925.56
17. $13.38
18. $6,341.71
19. $261.89
20. 0.534
21. 853.2
22. $464.91
23. 310.05
24. 135.8
25. 34,368.975
26. 0.0975
27. $8.23
28. about $320
29. The digits are the same; 23×368 has the greater product.

Page 13

1. 0.072
2. 0.0681
3. 0.4018
4. 0.990
5. 0.0140
6. 0.702
7. 947.394
8. 0.42
9. 1.7395
10. 339.69
11. 0.0588
12. 3.0105
13. 5.22
14. 1.3986
15. 0.1208
16. 118.047
17. 0.582
18. 0.0126
19. 0.7568
20. 0.432
21. 570
22. 0.81
23. 86
24. 95.6
25. 17,800
26. 4,569
27. 0.0288 cm
28. $8.18
29. The digits are the same, except for the number of zeros; 0.6×2.49 has the greater product.

Page 14

1. 3.2
2. 1.72
3. 3.8
4. 4.2
5. 2.32
6. 0.26
7. 3.2
8. 2.46
9. 1.08
10. 0.546
11. 5.1
12. 0.462
13. 2.7
14. 8.52
15. 5.25
16. 0.047
17. 2.07
18. 6.32
19. 52.7

20. $1,688.75
21. about 0.7 lb
22. Brand A, at $0.22 a skein

Page 15

1. 12.85
2. 2.595
3. 8.425
4. 0.65
5. 7.175
6. 0.316
7. 5.95
8. 7.405
9. 3.725
10. 0.505
11. 0.432
12. 3.57
13. 0.215
14. 0.365
15. 1.046
16. 0.456
17. 5.25 min
18. $52.00
19. $0.45
20. $0.55

Page 16

1. A. 48 and 12
   B. 4
   C. 480 and 120
   D. 4
   E. They are the same.
2. It has no effect.
3. 2
4. 6
5. 3
6. 3
7. 2
8. 2
9. same
10. different
11. same
12. different
13. same
14. different
15. same
16. different
17. different
18. different
19. same
20. different

Page 17

1. 7.3
2. 2.6
3. 37.6
4. 0.05
5. 7.6
6. 3.29
7. 34
8. 560
9. 0.64
10. 43.5
11. 54
12. 4.21
13. 6.655
14. 4,510
15. 6.5
16. 2.54
17. 3.22
18. 254
19. 36.9 hr
20. $42.16
21. 50 dimes

Page 18

1. 19
2. 15
3. 0.36
4. 59
5. 21
6. 2.2
7. 79
8. 6.1
9. 6.4
10. 24.5
11. 18.9
12. 9.1
13. 2.4
14. 20.4
15. 3.8
16. 160.9
17. 5.49
18. 6.85
19. 0.06
20. 2.29
21. 0.54
22. 11.67
21. 25.63
24. 21.72
25. $68.41
26. 5 times greater
27. Possible answer: 1 half dollar, 1 quarter, 4 dimes, 4 pennies

Page 19

1. B; the number of touchdowns in each game can vary.
2. B; the scores in each frame can vary.
3. A; the number of hours of television viewing each day can vary.
4. Possible answer: What was the highest test score recorded?
5. Possible answer: Which model was sold the least?
6. Possible answer: In which year was the least amount of waste recycled?
7. Possible answer: What was the highest daily low temperature?

Page 20

1. Possible answer: What is the median number of songs purchased?
2. There are peaks at 0–4 and 10–14.
3. There are no gaps in the data.
4. No; Possible explanation: there is no place you can draw a vertical line that separates the graph into two mirror images.
5. There are peaks at 6 and 8 students and gaps at 4 and 7 students. There are clusters from 0 to 3, at 5 and 6, and from 8 to 11.

Page 21

1–2. Answers and explanations will vary.
3. Check bar graph.
4. Check histogram.
5–6. Answers will vary.
7. Check problem.

Page 22

1. 5 stacks
2. 9 + 6 + 7 + 10 + 3 = 35
3. 7 cubes
4. 7 photographs
5. 35 ÷ 5 = 7
6. 29 + 58 + 84 = 171; 171 ÷ 3 = 57; 57 days

Page 23

1. 5, 7, 6
2. 35, 20, 33
3. 6, 7, 7
4. 26, 17, 27
5. 79, 48, 85
6. 102, 30, 109
7. 88
8. 91
9. 11, 19, 12
10. Answers will vary.

Page 24

1. 48, 54, 37, 37
2. 23, 88, 89, none
3. 31, 76, 77.5, 88
4. 56, 75, 84, 85
5. 29; 86; 90; 90, 94
6. 51; 70; 67; 56, 67
7. 78; 31
8. 80; 18
9. 210.54
10. 116.775
11. 26.46
12. 0.4728
13. 14.5
14. 105.25
15. 125.5
16. 931.0
17. 8.4
18. 6.45

Page 25

1. min $6.00; max $19.00
2. $15.50
3.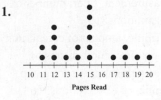
4. $13
5. $17
6. $2
7. Possible answer: No, although the mean is less than $16, there is only one item that costs less than $16.

Page 26

1. Less than; interquartile range; less than; interquartile range; warmer than; more than
2. Lake A: median 8 lb, range 8lb; Lake B: median 5.5 lb, range 3 lb; The fish in Lake A tend to weigh more than the fish in Lake B, and the fish weights in Lake A also vary more.

3. The average height in Class 2 is greater, and the heights of the students in Class 2 vary more.
4. Both sets of tests have a median of 80. The interquartile range of the math scores, 25, is greater than that of the science, which is 5.

Page 27

1.

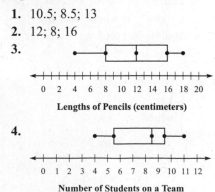

Pages Read

2. 15 pages; it has the tallest stack of dots on the dot plot.

3.

Pages Read	
Number of Pages	Frequency
10–13	7
14–17	9
18–21	4

4.

Pages Read		
Number of Pages	Frequency	Relative Frequency
10–13	7	35%
14–17	9	45%
18–21	4	20%

5. 55%

Page 28

1. 10.5; 8.5; 13
2. 12; 8; 16
3.

Lengths of Pencils (centimeters)

4.

Number of Students on a Team

5. $26; $20
6. 8 ounces

Page 29

1. Attribute: daily temperature; unit of measure: degrees Fahrenheit; means of measurement: thermometer; number of observations: 25
2. Attribute: height of plants; unit of measure: inches; means of measurement: ruler; number of observations: 10
3. Attribute: amount of cereal; unit of measure: cups; means of measurement: measuring cup; number of observations: 16
4. Attribute: weight of dogs; unit of measure: pounds; means of measurement: scale; number of observations: 8
5. clock or watch
6. miles per hour

Page 30

1. Yes; from 12 to 13, and at 17
2. There are clusters from 10 to 11, 14 to 16, and 18 to 19.
3. Possible answer: The dot plot shows that the restaurant sold from 10 to 19 omelets each day. There were usually 14 to 19 omelets sold each day.
4. 1 peak
5. The number of visitors starts high for 0 to 9 visitors, and then decreases for each interval.
6. Yes; there is a peak near the middle, and the two halves are mirror images.

Page 31

1. 1 hour
2. 4 inches
3. 1 year
4. 2.4 hours
5. 2 grams
6. 4.4°F

Page 32

1. 17, 1, 16, 16 miles
2. 12, 4, 8, 8 miles
3. 35
4. 20
5. 3.6 cm
6. 1.25 years
7. 2.4 minutes
8. $4

Page 33

1. 12; Possible answer: The outlier decreases the mean from about 25.3 to 24. The outlier decreases the median from 26 to 25.
2. $100; Possible answer: The outlier increases the mean from $22 to $31.75. The outlier increases the median from $20 to $22.
3. less; If Milton was injured before a game, he probably scored fewer points during the game.
4. The outlier is 60. It decreases the mean from about 94.8 to 87.8. It slightly decreases the median from 94.5 to 94.
5. The outlier is 96. It increases the mean from about 36 to about 48. It increases the median from 37 to 39.

Page 34

1. mean, 13 miles; median, 15 miles; mode, 16 miles; mean; mode; median
2.

Range, 10; interquartile range, 2; The interquartile range; most of the data values are from 1 to 3, so the interquartile range is a better description of the data set.
3. mean, 74.3; median, 85; mode, none; The median; there is no mode and the mean is less than almost all of the data values.
4. range, 8; interquartile range, 5; The range; there are several low values and also several high values.

Page 35

1. 5^2
2. 8^5
3. 9^3
4. 2^4
5. 7^6
6. $(2.3)^2$
7. 625
8. 169
9. 1.44
10. 1
11. 1,000,000
12. 49

13. 1,080 mi
14. 15 gal
15-18. Estimates may vary
15. 100
16. 8
17. 120
18. 40
19. 134,288
20. 176
21. 10.35
22. 75

Page 36

1. 20
2. 20^2
3. 20^3
4. 160,000
5. 3,200,000
6. 3
7. 2
8. 12
9. 25
10. 5
11. 33
12. 10,000,000
13. 10,000
14. 1,000
15. 1 googol of zeros

Page 37

1. prime
2. composite
3. prime
4. composite
5. composite
6. prime
7. composite
8. composite
9. 1, 2, 4, 8
10. 1, 3, 5, 15
11. 1, 2, 5, 10
12. 1, 2, 3, 4, 6, 8, 12, 24
13. 1, 5, 7, 35
14. 1, 2, 4, 7, 14, 28
15. 1, 2, 4, 5, 10, 20, 25, 50, 100
16. 1, 5, 13, 65
17. 1, 2, 5, 10, 25, 50
18. 1, 2, 17, 34
19. 1, 2, 4, 5, 8, 10, 20, 40
20. 1, 7, 11, 77
21. 1, 2, 3, 4, 6, 7, 12, 14, 21, 28, 42, 84
22. 1, 3, 5, 9, 15, 45
23. 1, 2, 23, 46

24. Possible answer: 2 and 10

25. 1 by 48; 2 by 24; 3 by 16; 4 by 12; 6 by 8

26. 47

27. 53

Page 38

1. prime
2. prime
3. composite
4. prime
5. composite
6. composite
7. 2×3^2
8. 2×17
9. $2^4 \times 3$
10. $2^3 \times 7$
11. 2^4
12. $2^3 \times 3^2$
13. 2×3^3
14. 2×29
15. $2^2 \times 3 \times 5$
16. $2^2 \times 5^2$
17. $2^2 \times 5 \times 7$
18. $2^3 \times 5^2$
19. 18
20. 315
21. 2,200
22. 735
23. 1,925
24. 76
25. 72
26. 2,079
27. 1,040
28. 9 choices
29. 23 and 29
30. 4, 9, 25, 49

Page 39

1. $2 \times 2 \times 11$
2. $2 \times 3 \times 3 \times 5$
3. $2 \times 2 \times 2 \times 2 \times 3$
4. $2 \times 2 \times 3 \times 17$
5. $2 \times 2 \times 2 \times 2 \times 5 \times 5$
6. $2 \times 2 \times 2 \times 7$
7. 99
8. 364
9. 54
10. $2 \times 2 \times 2 \times 2 \times 2 \times 5$
11. 237

Page 40

1–6. Check factor trees.

1. $2 \times 2 \times 5$
2. $3 \times 5 \times 5$
3. $3 \times 3 \times 7$
4. $2 \times 2 \times 2 \times 7$
5. $2 \times 3 \times 3$
6. $2 \times 3 \times 3 \times 3$
7. 2^4
8. $2^3 \times 3$
9. $2^2 \times 7$
10. $3^2 \times 5$
11. $2^3 \times 5$
12. $2^2 \times 3^2$
13. 20 students
14. 3
15. $2^2 \times 3^2 \times 5$, or 180
16. Possible answer: 2^2

Page 41

1. 1, 2, 7, 14
2. 1, 2, 3, 4, 6, 12
3. 1, 13
4. 1, 2, 3, 4, 6, 8, 12, 24
5. 1, 2, 3, 4, 6, 12, 18, 36
6. 1, 2, 4, 8, 16, 32
7. 1, 2, 4, 8, 16, 32, 64
8. 1, 7, 13, 91
9. 1, 2, 4, 8; 1, 2, 4, 8, 16; 1, 2, 4, 8
10. 1, 3, 9; 1, 2, 3, 4, 6, 8, 12, 24; 1, 3
11. 1, 2, 5, 10; 1, 3, 5, 15; 1, 5
12. 1, 2, 3, 4, 6, 12; 1, 13; 1
13. 1, 3, 9; 1, 3, 9, 27; 9
14. 1, 2, 3, 4, 6, 12; 1, 2, 3, 6, 9, 18; 6
15. 1, 13; 1, 3, 13, 39; 13
16. 1, 2, 7, 14; 1, 3, 7, 21; 7
17. 1
18. 1
19. 1
20. 1
21. Answers will vary. Possible answers; All the pairs are prime numbers. The only common factor is 1.

Page 42

1. 1, 2
2. 1, 2, 3, 6
3. 1, 2, 3, 6
4. 1, 3, 5, 15
5. 1, 2, 5, 10
6. 1, 5
7. 2
8. 2
9. 7

10. 9
11. 5
12. 4
13. 15
14. 6
15. 6
16. 3
17. 3
18. 18
19. 18 inches
20. apron
21. 6
22. 2
23. 2
24. 32
25. 49
26. $\frac{3}{7} > \frac{2}{7} > \frac{1}{7}$
27. $\frac{4}{5} > \frac{2}{3} > \frac{1}{2}$
28. $\frac{3}{12} > \frac{1}{6} > \frac{1}{8}$
29. 1, 2, 4, 8
30. 1, 2, 4, 7, 14, 28
31. 1, 2, 3, 6, 9, 18, 27, 54

Page 43

1. 8, 12, 16
2. 16, 24, 32
3. 20, 30, 40
4. 6, 9, 12
5. 10, 15, 20
6. 14, 21, 28
7. 22, 33, 44
8. 12, 18, 24
9. 18, 27, 36
10. 24, 36, 48
11. 40
12. 12
13. 28
14. 63
15. 30
16. 24
17. 84
18. 40
19. 21
20. 35
21. 6
22. 12
23. 24
24. 18
25. 9
26. 6 minutes after they start
27. 28 apples
28. 4 and 6
29. 2 and 8

155

Page 44

1. 12, 24
2. 4, 8
3. 10, 20
4. $\frac{3}{12}, \frac{10}{12}$
5. $\frac{2}{4}, \frac{1}{4}$
6. $\frac{4}{10}, \frac{3}{10}$
7. $\frac{6}{8}, \frac{1}{8}$
8. $\frac{12}{30}, \frac{5}{30}$
9. $\frac{9}{24}, \frac{2}{24}$
10. $\frac{8}{14}, \frac{3}{14}$
11. $\frac{27}{36}, \frac{8}{36}$
12. $\frac{1}{9}, \frac{6}{9}$
13. $\frac{20}{24}, \frac{9}{24}$
14. $\frac{8}{18}, \frac{2}{18}$
15. $\frac{18}{42}, \frac{14}{42}$
16. Possible answer: $\frac{1}{2}, \frac{1}{5}$

Page 45

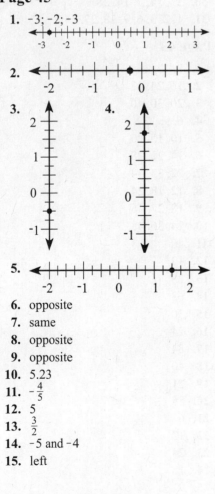

1. -3; -2; -3
2.
3.
4.
5.
6. opposite
7. same
8. opposite
9. opposite
10. 5.23
11. $-\frac{4}{5}$
12. 5
13. $\frac{3}{2}$
14. -5 and -4
15. left

Page 46

1. $\frac{13}{25}$
2. $\frac{1}{50}$
3. $4\frac{4}{5}$
4. $6\frac{1}{40}$
5. 0.68; terminates
6. $0.\overline{7}$; repeats
7. 4.65; terminates
8. $7.\overline{72}$ repeats
9. 0.4; $\frac{2}{5}$
10. 1.9; $1\frac{9}{10}$
11. 1.2; $1\frac{1}{5}$
12. 0.6; $\frac{3}{5}$
13. 0.625
14. $\frac{4}{5}$

Page 47

1. <; left; less than
2. >
3. >
4. <
5. <
6. <
7. >
8. -1.7; -1; 0.2
9. $-2\frac{3}{4}; -1\frac{3}{4}; -\frac{3}{5}$
10. -2.7; $-1\frac{2}{3}$; -0.5
11. 0; $-\frac{5}{6}$; -1
12. 1.82; $\frac{4}{5}$; $-\frac{2}{5}$
13. 1.1; -2.19; -2.5
14. -15 m > -20.5 m
15. $78 > -$42
16. -31 points < -30 points
17. Frosty Town
18. Any amount from -$20.99 to -$20.01.

Page 48

1. =
2. >
3. <
4. >
5. >
6. =
7. <
8. =
9. <
10. =
11. <
12. >; >

13–18. Answers will vary. One possible answer given.

13. $5 \times 6 - 3$
14. $5 \times 3 - 6 \div 3$
15. $6 \times 3 + 6 \times 5$
16. $8x + 4$
17. $3x - 5 = 2$
18. $2x + 1 \geq 3$
19. $\frac{1}{100}$
20. $68
21. 11.7333
22. 136.521
23. 0.54

Page 49

1. 2 blocks west, 4 blocks north
2. 3 blocks east, 1 block south
3. 1 block east, 2 blocks south
4. 3 blocks east, 3 blocks north
5. 3 blocks west, 1 block south
6–11. Check map.
12. Check story.

Page 50

1. (1, 4)
2. (-2, 3)
3. (-2, -2)
4. (3, 2)
5. (1, -1)
6. (-2, 0)
7. (-4, 1)
8. (3, 0)
9–16. Check graph.
17. (2, 0)
18. Possible answer: (1, 2)
19. They would be the same.

Page 51

1. IV
2. III
3. I
4. II
5. IV
6. II
7. y
8. x
9. x
10. (6, -10)
11. (-11, -3)
12. (8, -2)
13. Quadrant I
14. y-axis

156

Page 52

1. $(1, \frac{1}{2})$
2. $(-1, -2\frac{1}{2})$
3. $(2, -1\frac{1}{2})$
4. $(-1\frac{1}{2}, 0)$
5. $(-2, 2\frac{1}{2})$
6. $(1\frac{3}{4}, 1\frac{1}{2})$
7.
8.
9.
10.
11.
12.
13.
14.

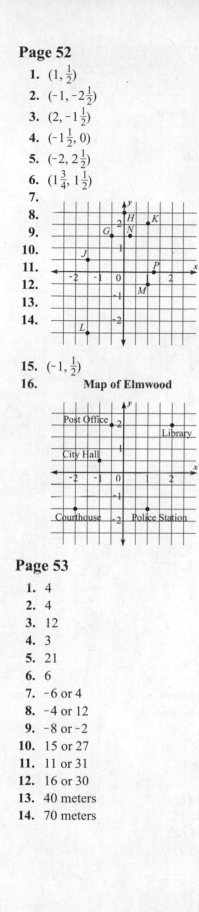

15. $(-1, \frac{1}{2})$
16.

Map of Elmwood

Page 53

1. 4
2. 4
3. 12
4. 3
5. 21
6. 6
7. -6 or 4
8. -4 or 12
9. -8 or -2
10. 15 or 27
11. 11 or 31
12. 16 or 30
13. 40 meters
14. 70 meters

Page 54

1. 3; 2; 3, 2, 5
2. 4;

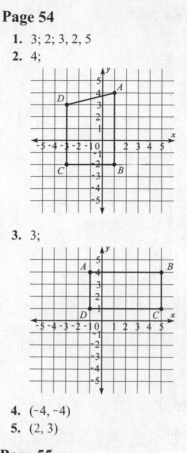

3. 3;

4. $(-4, -4)$
5. $(2, 3)$

Page 55

1. $37 + 45 = 82$; 82 pictures
2. $348 \times 12 = 4{,}176$; 4,176 min
3. $63 \times 4 = 252$; 252 sandwiches
4. $40 \div 8 = 5$; 5 people
5. $60 \div 5 = 12$; 12 people
6. $28 \times 3 = 84$; 84 people
7. 126 miles
8. about 5 grams

Page 56

1. $7p$, where p is the number of pumpkins
2. $210
3. $\frac{h}{12}$, where h is the height of the building
4. 11 floors
5. $100 \div (b + 24)$; 4; $3\frac{1}{3}$; $2.\overline{6}$
6. $5m + 13$; 18; 43; 80.5
7. $16s$; s is the number of months
8. 144 days

Page 57

1–4. Equations may vary.
1. $68 + m = 116; $48
2. $a - 9 = 46$; 55 years old
3. $1\frac{1}{2} + n = 2\frac{1}{4}$; $\frac{3}{4}$ cup
4. $c - $550 = $1{,}360$; $1,910

5. 12 years old
6. 9 m
7. Check problem.

Page 58

1. 9
2. 14
3. One $\frac{3}{4}$-pt container can be filled with $\frac{3}{16}$ pt left over.
4. $\frac{1}{5}$ pound

Page 59

1. 4; 8 pumpkin muffins and 7 banana muffins
2. 2 cards; 8 groups of soccer cards and 11 groups of baseball cards
3. 10 chairs; 5 rows of black chairs and 6 rows of white chairs
4. 6 teaspoons; 3 teaspoons of cinnamon and 5 teaspoons of nutmeg
5. 8 counters; 3 bags of blue counters and 7 bags of yellow counters

Page 60

1. $(6, 0)$
2. $(5, -6)$
3. 14 blocks
4. 10 blocks
5. $(0, 3)$
6. $(-6, 4)$
7. 6 miles

Page 61

1. 35%
2. 85%
3. no
4. No. The total surveyed would then be 110, not 100.
5. 12%
6. 45%
7. 41%
8. 80%; $\frac{40}{50} = \frac{80}{100}$
9. $1.20
10. In most cases, it is higher with the milk added.

Page 62

1. 5 fives
2. 3 fours
3. 4 threes
4. $\frac{8}{10} \div \frac{4}{10} = 2$
5. $\frac{12}{3} \div \frac{2}{3} = 6$
6. $\frac{8}{10} \div \frac{2}{10} = 4$

157

7. 2
8. 2
9. 3
10. 2
11. 3
12. 1
13. 3
14. 1
15. 3
16. 4
17. 3
18. 5
19. 32,000 miles

Page 63

1. 4, 4
2. 4, 4
3. 3, 3
4. $\frac{2}{5}$, $\frac{2}{5}$
5. 1
6. 3
7. $\frac{5}{2}$
8. $\frac{1}{4}$
9. $\frac{1}{5}$
10. $\frac{3}{2}$
11. 7
12. $\frac{9}{2}$
13. $\frac{8}{3}$
14. 8
15. $\frac{7}{5}$
16. $\frac{5}{3}$
17. 16
18. $\frac{3}{2}$
19. $\frac{5}{4}$
20. 20
21. $3\frac{1}{3}$; $\frac{5}{1}$, $3\frac{1}{3}$
22. 4; $\frac{6}{1}$, 4
23. $\frac{5}{6}$, $\frac{4}{3}$, $\frac{5}{6}$
24. $\frac{3}{14}$, $\frac{3}{2}$, $\frac{3}{14}$
25. $1\frac{13}{15}$; $\frac{7}{3}$, $1\frac{13}{15}$
26. $3\frac{1}{3}$; $\frac{4}{1}$, $3\frac{1}{3}$
27. $\frac{27}{64}$, $\frac{9}{8}$, $\frac{27}{64}$
28. $1\frac{5}{9}$; $\frac{7}{2}$, $1\frac{5}{9}$
29. $2\frac{2}{7}$; $\frac{4}{1}$, $2\frac{2}{7}$
30. $2\frac{3}{16}$; $\frac{5}{2}$, $2\frac{3}{16}$
31. $1\frac{1}{2}$; $\frac{5}{1}$, $1\frac{1}{2}$
32. $1\frac{2}{3}$; $\frac{5}{2}$, $1\frac{2}{3}$
33. 4

Page 64

1. $\frac{2}{3}$
2. $\frac{4}{1}$, $\frac{32}{1}$
3. 4, $\frac{5}{1}$
4. $\frac{5}{3}$, $\frac{5}{9}$
5. > 1
6. > 1
7. < 1
8. > 1
9. > 1
10. > 1
11. < 1
12. > 1
13. $12\frac{1}{2}$
14. $12\frac{1}{2}$
15. $1\frac{1}{6}$
16. $1\frac{3}{4}$
17. 21
18. 16
19. 9
20. $2\frac{2}{3}$
21. 10
22. $2\frac{1}{10}$
23. $4\frac{4}{5}$
24. $1\frac{1}{3}$
25. $1\frac{2}{3}$
26. $2\frac{2}{5}$
27. $1\frac{2}{3}$
28. $\frac{11}{24}$
29. $\frac{4}{5}$
30. 8
31. 2
32. $\frac{4}{5}$
33. $6\frac{2}{3}$ servings
34. 90 times
35. 5

Page 65

1. 9
2. 20
3. 15;
4. 3;
5. $1\frac{3}{8}$;
6. $1\frac{1}{9}$;
7. $1\frac{2}{5}$ quarts
8. 14

Page 66

1. $\frac{9}{4} \times \frac{8}{1}$
2. $\frac{5}{6} \times \frac{2}{3}$
3. $\frac{7}{3} \times \frac{1}{4}$
4. $\frac{6}{5} \times \frac{3}{17}$
5. $3\frac{1}{8}$
6. $5\frac{2}{5}$
7. $\frac{1}{4}$
8. $1\frac{9}{35}$
9. $\frac{16}{39}$
10. $2\frac{6}{11}$
11. $2\frac{3}{16}$
12. $2\frac{2}{3}$
13. 9
14. $2\frac{4}{7}$
15. $1\frac{2}{3}$
16. 6
17. $1\frac{1}{2}$
18. 3
19. $1\frac{3}{13}$
20. $4\frac{1}{3}$
21. 18
22. $\frac{5}{9}$
23. $\frac{7}{12}$
24. $\frac{9}{25}$
25. 8 pieces
26. 6 hours
27. < 1
28. > 1
29. > 1
30. < 1
31. 0.405
32. 47.15
33. 51.642
34. 60.72
35. $\frac{3}{5}$
36. $16\frac{4}{5}$
37. $3\frac{3}{8}$
38. $5\frac{19}{27}$
39. $1\frac{1}{4}$

158

40. $6\frac{1}{2}$

41. $\frac{1}{6}$

42. $19\frac{1}{5}$

Page 67

1. 20; 200; 2,000
2. 10; 100; 1,000
3. 200; 20; 2
4. 0.005
5. 0.006
6. 0.003
7. 0.125
8. 0.00025
9. 3.6
10. 970
11. 3
12. 34
13. 9,000
14. 2,100
15. 0.001
16. 76
17. 350
18. 14,000
19. 3,900
20. 40
21. 6,300
22. 1.75 L
23. 130,000 g
24. yes; 750 mL = 0.75 L and 0.75 L × 2 = 1.5 L

Page 68

1. 0.003
2. 240
3. 1.35
4. 20,000
5. 0.0004
6. 0.31
7. 35,000
8. 5,700
9. 20
10. 33
11. 3,600
12. 0.56
13. 45
14. 0.0065
15. 0.78
16. 35.05
17. 6,800
18. 0.026
19. 0.23
20. 0.047
21. 240

22. 177,000
23. 456,000
24. 1,760
25. 16 marbles
26. 0.72 kg
27. 47.9 kg
28. 4 glasses
29. Yes; there would be six 400 mL servings.

Page 69

1–6. One possible estimate is given.
1. 400
2. 1,000
3. 1,800
4. 7
5. 2,000
6. 200,000
7. multiply by 12; 432 in.
8. divide by 5,280; 4 mi
9. divide by 3; 22 yd
10. 115; 1
11. 1; 2,720
12. 81; 2
13. 7,040
14. $\frac{2}{3}$
15. $\frac{1}{3}$
16. $7\frac{1}{6}$
17. $10\frac{2}{3}$ yd
18. 78 in.
19. No. There are 5,280 ft in one mile, but each brick is shorter than 1 ft. More bricks are needed.

Page 70

1. 24
2. 4
3. 3
4. 128
5. 131
6. 1,000
7. 10
8. 28
9. 4
10. 18
11. $\frac{3}{4}$
12. 2
13. $1\frac{1}{2}$
14. $8\frac{1}{2}$
15. 100
16. 25
17. 260
18. 5,000

19. yes
20. $11\frac{1}{4}$ tons
21. the second week
22. 70 pounds
23. blouses
24. Yes. She used 88 ft of fabric, which is $29\frac{1}{3}$ yd.

Page 71

1. hexagonal prism; 12, 18, 8
2. triangular pyramid; 4, 6, 4
3. cube; 8, 12, 6
4. triangular prism; 6, 9, 5
5. 2 circles, 1 rectangle
6. 1 square, 4 triangles
7. 6 rectangles
8. triangular pyramid
9. The number of edges is 2 less than the sum of the faces and vertices.
10. square pyramid
11. Kasa, Louisiana; Lola, Kentucky; Leroy, Iowa

Page 72

1. rectangular pyramid, or square pyramid
2. octagonal prism
3. cone
4. triangular prism
5. pentagonal pyramid
6–7. Answers will vary.
8. 8,650 g
9. 0.220 L
10. 72 in.
11. 3 lb
12. 160 oz
13. 10 pt
14. 24 oz

Page 73

1. pentagonal pyramid
2. triangular pyramid
3. cylinder
4. pentagonal prism
5. cylinder, no
6. triangular pyramid, yes
7. cube or rectangular prism, yes
8. triangular prism, yes
9. 7, 10, 15
10. 6, 6, 10
11. 10, 16, 24
12. 9, 9, 16
13. 6, 2; 4, 5; 1, 3

159

Page 74

1. pyramid; rectangular pyramid
2. pyramid; triangular pyramid
3. pyramid; pentagonal pyramid
4. prism; hexagonal prism
5. 2 square bases; other faces parallelograms
6. 2 triangular bases; other faces parallelograms
7. 2 rectangular bases; other faces parallelograms
8. 40 inches or 3 feet 4 inches
9. rectangular prism; television will not fit in pyramid
10. c

Page 75

1. 3 to 2; 3:2; $\frac{3}{2}$
2. 2 to 14; 2:14; $\frac{2}{14}$ or 1 to 7; 1:7; $\frac{1}{7}$
3. 5 to 4; 5:4; $\frac{5}{4}$
4. 4 to 5; 4:5; $\frac{4}{5}$
5. 14 to 5; 14:5; $\frac{14}{5}$
6. 4 to 2; 4:2; $\frac{4}{2}$
7. part to part
8. part to whole
9. part to part
10. part to part
11. whole to part
12. part to part
13. 8:10 or 4:5
14. 20:30 or 2:3
15. 1:3

Page 76

1–4. Check drawings.
1. 3 green circles: 4 purple circles
2. 2 red hats: 3 blue hats
3. 5 trees: 2 flowers
4. 1 dog: 4cats
5. 12:5; $\frac{12}{5}$
6. $\frac{6}{7}$; six to seven
7. 15:21; $\frac{15}{21}$
8. 8:3; eight to three
9. $\frac{40}{3}$; forty to three
10. 7:18; seven to eighteen
11. 6:11
12. 8:3
13. 29:54

Page 77

1–8. Answers will vary. One possible answer is given.
1. 3:1.99
2. 2.99:12
3. 26:1
4. 45:1
5. 2.50: 4
6. 1:7
7. 55:1
8. 2:12
9. $0.20 each
10. $0.13 each
11. 31 mi per gal
12. $0.50 per lb
13. $38 per hour
14. $3.65 each
15. $5 each
16. $22.50 per hour
17. $3.20
18. $1.25
19. about $36
20. 7.6 gal
21. Ben

Page 78

1. $\frac{15}{5} = \frac{\square}{2}$; 6 yd
2. $\frac{42}{6} = \frac{14}{\square}$; 2 wk
3. $\frac{16}{4} = \frac{\square}{2}$; 8 eggs
4. $\frac{6}{30} = \frac{8}{\square}$; 40 min
5. $\frac{50}{2} = \frac{\square}{3}$; $75
6. $\frac{150}{2} = \frac{\square}{1}$; 75 km
7. $\frac{230 \text{ mi}}{1 \text{ day}}$
8. $\frac{\$15}{1 \text{ day}}$
9. $\frac{20 \text{ flowers}}{1 \text{ bouquet}}$
10. $\frac{30 \text{ beads}}{1 \text{ necklace}}$
11. $\frac{\$6}{1 \text{ hr}}$
12. $\frac{28 \text{ mi}}{1 \text{ gal}}$
13. $\frac{86 \text{ km}}{1 \text{ hr}}$
14. $\frac{\$0.38}{1 \text{ L}}$
15. $\frac{14.5 \text{ mi}}{1 \text{ hr}}$
16. 11 mi
17. 1 mi
18. One possible answer is: If it takes 72 tokens to play 12 games, how many tokens are needed to play 10 games?

Page 79

1–6. Answers may vary. Possible answers are given.
1. 6:10; 9:15
2. 8:10; 12:15
3. 2:14; 3:21
4. 2:3; 12:18
5. $\frac{1}{5}$, $\frac{4}{20}$
6. $\frac{3}{9}$, $\frac{12}{36}$
7. no
8. yes
9. no
10. yes
11. yes
12. no
13–14. Answers may vary.
13. $\frac{3}{8} \times \frac{2}{2} = \frac{6}{16}$; $\frac{3}{8} \times \frac{3}{3} = \frac{9}{24}$
14. $\frac{12}{18} \div \frac{2}{2} = \frac{6}{9}$; $\frac{12}{18} \div \frac{3}{3} = \frac{4}{6}$
15. 4:12; 8:24; yes
16. 4 bananas, 10 apples
17. 36 hours, 18 hours

Page 80

1–8. Answers will vary.
1. $\frac{4}{6}$, $\frac{6}{9}$
2. 8:10; 12:15
3. 10 to 12; 15 to 18
4. 16:10; 24:15
5. 6 to 2; 9 to 3
6. $\frac{12}{14}$, $\frac{18}{21}$
7. $\frac{18}{4}$, $\frac{27}{6}$
8. 8 to 18; 12 to 27
9. yes
10. no
11. yes
12. no
13. yes
14. no
15. yes
16. yes
17. 10
18. 1
19. 12
20. 40
21. 1
22. 24
23. 6
24. 5
25. 6 books
26. $66.00
27. 265 min or 4 hr 25 min

Answer Key

Core Skills Math, Grade 6

Page 81

1. $\dfrac{1,800°}{5\text{ revolutions}}, \dfrac{360°}{1\text{ revolution}}$
2. $\dfrac{312\text{ cards}}{6\text{ decks}}, \dfrac{52\text{ cards}}{1\text{ deck}}$
3. $\dfrac{18.6\text{ miles}}{3\text{ hours}}, \dfrac{6.2\text{ miles}}{1\text{ hour}}$
4. $\dfrac{\$30.16}{8\text{ pounds}}, \dfrac{\$3.77}{1\text{ pound}}$
5. the 5-game package
6. Tom
7. Savoy
8. the second company
9. 512 miles per hour
10. $2.09 per pound

Page 82

1. Yes, $\frac{4}{6}$ is equivalent to $\frac{8}{12}$.
2. No, $\frac{5}{3}$ is not equivalent to $\frac{9}{6}$.
3. Yes, $\frac{4}{5}$ is equivalent to $\frac{8}{10}$.
4. No, $\frac{10}{7}$ is not equivalent to $\frac{15}{12}$.

Page 83

1. 8, 16, 24, 32, 40;
   3, 4, 5
2. 8, 16, (3, 24), (4, 32), (5, 40)
3. **Christie's Bracelets**

4. 8 charms are needed if 1 bracelet is made.
5. 10, 20, 30, 40
6. $\dfrac{10\text{ bars}}{1\text{ box}}$
7. 56 charms
8. 9 boxes

Page 84

1. 4:6, 4 to 6, or $\frac{4}{6}$
2. 2:3, 2 to 3, $\frac{2}{3}$
3. The ratios are equivalent.
4. $\frac{4}{6} = \frac{2}{3}$
5. The cross products are equal.
6. $\frac{6}{8}$ or $\frac{3}{4}$
7. $\frac{6}{4}$ or $\frac{3}{2}$
8. $\frac{8}{6}$ or $\frac{4}{3}$
9. $\frac{4}{6}$ or $\frac{2}{3}$

10. $\frac{5}{4}$
11. $\frac{5}{8}$
12. $\frac{28}{6}$ or $\frac{14}{3}$

Page 85

1. 14
2. 7
3. 6
4. 4

5–8. Check drawings.

5. 18
6. 3.5
7. 4
8. 35
9. 72 fluid ounces
10. 15 baskets

Page 86

1. June
2. 7th meeting
3. 9th year
4. April
5. 256 pieces
6. The house number is 567.

Page 87

1. $\frac{20}{100}$, 0.20, 20%
2. $\frac{78}{100}$, 0.78, 78%
3. 29%
4. 2%
5. 75%
6. 95%
7. 37%
8. 11%
9. $\frac{54}{100}$, 0.54
10. $1.82
11. 26%; 64%

Page 88

1. 0.85
2. 0.03
3. 0.95
4. 0.17
5. 0.68
6. 0.162
7. 0.04
8. 1.55
9. 0.50
10. 0.715
11. 0.888
12. 1.03
13. 6%
14. 78%

15. 143%
16. 60.7%
17. 52%
18. 11%
19. 109%
20. 140.6%
21. 165%
22. 10.12; 1,012%
23. 37.8; 3,780%
24. 0.82
25. 351 mi
26. $\frac{28}{15} \div \frac{7}{5}, \frac{7}{5} \div \frac{28}{15}$

Page 89

1. $\frac{71}{100}$
2. $\frac{3}{100}$
3. $\frac{41}{10}$ or $4\frac{1}{10}$
4. $\frac{8}{5}$ or $1\frac{3}{5}$
5. $\frac{14}{25}$
6. $\frac{33}{50}$
7. $\frac{39}{50}$
8. $\frac{21}{25}$
9. $\frac{7}{25}$
10. 11%
11. 75%
12. 63%
13. 70%
14. 192%
15. 97%
16. 70%
17. $62\frac{1}{2}$%
18. 88%
19. 80%
20. $\frac{9}{50}$
21. $\frac{21}{100}$
22. 3%
23. yes
24. no
25. yes
26. yes
27. $0.30
28. $50
29. 42 mi
30. $11.50

Page 90

1. 85%
2. 42%
3. 12%
4. 9%
5. 93%
6. 79%

161

7. 3%
8. 97%
9. 49%
10. 53%
11. 15%
12. 50%
13. 20%
14. 200%
15. 75%
16. 90%
17. 36%
18. 16%
19. 5%
20. 167%
21. 40%
22. 212.5%
23. 75%
24. 60%
25. extra-small
26. 45%
27. 50%; draw perpendicular dotted lines to show that 4 of 8 congruent triangles are shaded.

Page 91
1. 0.14
2. $\frac{8}{100}$ or $\frac{2}{25}$
3. 18
4. 20
5. 40
6. 104
7. 315
8. 18
9. 105
10. 120
11. 7
12. 18
13. 8
14. 1,800
15. 8
16. 60
17. 11
18. 18
19. 27
20. 112
21. 21
22. 75
23. 8
24. 180
25. 9
26. 130
27. 6.75
28. 12.6
29. 72

30. 7.8
31. 10.5
32. 46.24
33. 168
34. 50.4
35. 374
36. 11.2
37. 89.1
38. 237.6
39. Answers will vary. Possible answers: sales tax, discount price, interest.

Page 92
1. 80
2. 15
3. 90
4. 12
5. 100
6. 1.4
7. 32
8. 45
9. 0.5
10. $0.80
11. 20
12. $2.10
13. $30
14. $3.56
15. $4.56
16. 100
17. 110
18. 14
19. 80%
20. 528 people
21. 1, 2, 4, 5, 10, or 20 cassettes
22. 6 cards
23. $15/1 pillow
24. 15 pages/1 h
25. 25 mi/1 gal
26. yes
27. no
28. yes
29. no
30. 45%
31. 60%
32. 66%
33. 25%

Page 93
1. 1.2
2. 127.5
3. 15
4. 72
5. 67.2

6. 37.8
7. 13.5
8. 103.6
9. 1.26
10. 9.8
11. 32.4
12. 180
13. $70
14. 33.8
15. 0.323
16. $4.50
17. about 28.26 in.
18. $472.80
19. $517.13

Page 94
1. 40
2. 500
3. 40
4. 200
5. 56
6. 600
7. 12
8. 100
9. 500
10. 1,600
11. $12,000
12. 85¢
13. $1.55, $13.95
14. $16.00, $16.00

Page 95
1–3. Estimates may vary.
1. c
2. c
3. a
4–12. Estimates may vary.
4. 50%
5. 28%
6. 25%
7. 12%
8. $33\frac{1}{3}$%
9. 25%
10. 50%
11. 50%
12. 50%
13. 200
14. 80
15. 70%
16. 15%
17. 75
18. $28

Page 96

1. 30; 75; 96
2. c
3. a
4. b
5. a
6. Answers will vary.

Page 97

1. 80
2. 160
3. 720
4. 200
5. 190
6. 200
7. 250
8. 500
9. 670
10. 58
11. 102.5
12. 100
13. 250
14. 2.8
15. 2,500
16. 125
17. 70
18. 220
19. 8,500 students
20. 30.25 hr
21. 120
22. 6
23. 50
24. 22.5
25. 8.72
26. 1.26

Page 98

1. 16 m²
2. 45 yd²
3. 28 cm²
4. 13.12 in.²
5. 13.87 m²
6. 4.84 ft²
7. 21 cm²
8. 44 mm²
9. 30 in.²
10. 168 yd²
11. 32 ft²
12. 4.5 m²
13. 1,410 ft²
14. 35.28 cm²
15. 6 yd²
16. 180 ft²
17. 36 ft
18. $107.40
19. 9 cm
20. 0.8 ft

Page 99

1. 6 cm²
2. 8 cm²
3. 8 mi²
4. 18 m²
5. 4 cm²
6. 21 ft²
7. 63 in.²
8. 48 m²
9. 85 ft²
10. 322 in.²
11. 2,880 m²
12. The triangle has the greater area because the bases of the two figures have equal lengths, but the height of the triangle is more than twice the height of the parallelogram.

Page 100

1. 24 cm²
2. 280 ft²
3. 4 cm²
4. 10 in.²
5. 12 ft²
6. 25.2 m²
7. 15.12 yd²
8. 7.31 cm²
9. 54 in.²
10. 440 mm²
11. 4 cm²
12. 8.17 m²
13. 0.495 ft²
14. 1.875 m²
15. 12 cm
16. 36.87
17. $10\frac{9}{10}$
18. 6.874
19. $3\frac{1}{2}$
20. 12.34
21. $3\frac{3}{4}$

Page 101

1. 90 ft²
2. 50 m
3. 10 mi
4. $20.25
5. about 8:40 A.M.
6. 64 cards
7. Answers will vary.

Page 102

1. 112 yd²
2. 252 cm²
3. 80 m²
4–5. Estimates may vary. One possible estimate is given.
4. 28 units²
5. 18 units²
6. about 23 cm²
7. Joy; 100 ft² bigger
8. The shaded figure must have a smaller area because it takes up only part of the space the triangle takes up. The shaded figure can have a greater perimeter because the distance around it can be greater than the distance around the triangle.

Page 103

1. 24 m²
2. 49 ft²
3. 40 in.²
4. 18 in.²
5. 96 m²
6. 62.98 m²
7. 40 m²
8. 66 m²
9. 140 in.²
10. Yes, if either the length or width respectively do not exceed the length and width of the hall.
11. Check answer.

Page 104

1. 12 cm²
2. 25 ft²
3. 18 cm²
4. 54 m²
5. 45 m²
6. 172 m²
7. 130 m²
8. 6 ft²
9. Check designs.

Page 105

1. 5 faces
2. 25 cm²
3. 12.5 cm²
4. 50 cm²
5. 75 cm²
6. 6 faces

Answer Key
Core Skills Math, Grade 6

7. 64 cm^2
8. by multiplying 64 cm^2 by 6
9. 384 cm^2
10. 22 m^2
11. 127.5 cm^2
12. 120 in.^{2}
13. Not necessarily. The six faces of figure A could have much smaller areas than the five faces of figure B, so figure A could have the smaller surface area.

Page 106

1. 69 cm^2
2. 77.98 m^2
3. 144 m^2
4. 233.63 cm^2
5. 32.64 in.^{2}
6. 142.8 m^2
7. 67.5 m^2
8. 4 gallons of paint
9. 946,015 ft^2

Page 107

1. $6\frac{3}{4}$ cubic units
2. 225 cubic units
3. 1550 cubic units
4. $22\frac{1}{2}$ cubic units
5. $16\frac{1}{2}$ cubic units
6. $28\frac{1}{8}$ cubic units
7. $31\frac{1}{2}$ in.^{3}
8. $49\frac{1}{2}$ ft^3

Page 108

1. $150\frac{5}{16}$ m^3
2. $27\frac{1}{2}$ in.^{3}
3. $91\frac{1}{8}$ mm^3
4. $112\frac{1}{2}$ ft^3
5. 36 m^3
6. $30\frac{3}{8}$ ft^3
7. $964\frac{1}{4}$ m^3
8. $\frac{1}{27}$ in.^{3}
9. 168 cm^3
10. 10 in.
11. 374 in.^{3}

Page 109

1. 6;
2. -3;
3. -10;
4. 8;
5. -60; no change in account balance
6. 12: neither gaining nor losing points
7. 25; no change in elevation
8. 20
9. -4
10. -95
11. 63
12. -25 points
13. 25 points

Page 110

1. down 4 floors
2. 8 feet down
3. 2-inch fall
4. loss of $10
5. -3; up 3 flights of stairs; +3
6. -25; 25 ft above sea level; +25
7. +10; a weight loss of 10 lb; -10
8. +45; a loss of $45; -45
9. -8; 8 degrees above zero; +8
10. +6; climb down 6 m; -6
11. + 8; -8
12. the same as before the increase
13. +2; -8
14. -282
15. $\frac{1}{2}$
16. $\frac{9}{2}$ or $4\frac{1}{2}$
17. 3
18. 63%
19. 50% or 0.5
20. 0.07

Page 111

1. -4
2. +1
3. -2
4. -7
5. +4
6. +7
7. -5
8. -1
9. >
10. <
11. >
12. >
13. -7 < -6 < -2 < 0
14. -7 < -6 < 4 < 5
15. -11 < -1 < 0 < 5 < 11
16. -8 < -7 < -6 < -3 < 0
17. Marshall City
18. Mr. Molina's house
19. -3 and 3

Page 112

1. <
2. <
3. =
4. >
5. >
6. >
7. =
8. <
9. <
10. =
11. <
12. <
13. <
14. >
15. >
16. =
17. =
18. >
19. >
20. =
21. -6 < 0 < 5
22. -20 < 17 < 18
23. -47 < 0 < 74
24. -6 < -4 < 4
25. 8 > 1 > -6
26. 44 > -13 > -31
27. 0 > -2 > -9
28. 7 > 0 > -5

Page 113

1. 7
2. 0
3. 17
4. 22
5. 6
6. 9
7. 8
8. 13
9. 12
10. 19
11. 11
12. 26
13. 18
14. 3
15. 10
16. 15
17. 23, -23

18. 14, -14
19. 32, -32
20. 29, -29
21. 21, -21
22. 40, -40
23. 12, -12
24. 99, -99

Page 114

1. -27
2. 20
3. -4
4. 4
5. 55
6. 143
7. 0
8. 91
9. 234
10. -145
11. 81
12. biking west 3 km
13. earning $25
14. falling 5°C
15. <
16. >
17. <
18. =
19. -5, -3, 2, 3
20. -17, -5, -2, 17
21. -10, -7, 2, 4, 5
22. 20, -20
23. 6:00 P.M. to midnight
24. -273.15

Page 115

1. 5; fewer
2. more
3. Carissa; an increase of $15
4. <
5. =
6. <
7. >
8. <
9. =
10. $55; more
11. Answers will vary. Possible answers -2, -1.

Page 116

1. $25 + t$ or $t + 25$
2. $110.1 - r$
3. $x - 13$
4. $100 - y$
5. $4.3 + d$ or $d + 4.3$
6. $q + 67$ or $67 + q$

7–12. Word expressions may vary. One possible answer is given.

7. 43 more than a number, k
8. y less than 15
9. v more than 3.4
10. 54 less than a number, a
11. t more than 34
12. x more than 8.7
13. $p + 10$ or $10 + p$
14. $s - 15$
15. 180 points
16. $2,200,000
17. Check problem.

Page 117

1–10. Word expressions may vary. One possible answer is given.

1. 7 fewer than x
2. 9 more than u
3. 6 more than w
4. 12 fewer than m
5. q fewer than 5
6. 6 times n
7. 15 times t
8. c divided by 4
9. 8 more than v
10. 7 times p
11. $t + 10$ or $10 + t$
12. $y + 6 = 8$ or $6 + y = 8$
13. negative seven plus m
14. $w - 10 = 15$
15. $t \div 5$ or $\frac{t}{5}$
16. $12 = 3f$
17. 5 years old
18. $n + \$0.50$
19. 5

Page 118

1. yz
2. $e - f$
3. $p + q$
4. $b \div 7$ or $\frac{b}{7}$
5. $r + 2$
6. $a - 6$
7. $12 \div n$ or $\frac{12}{n}$
8. $3n$
9. $n - 8$
10. $n + 1$
11. $100n$
12. $20 - n$
13. $32 - t$
14. $7n$
15. $28 \div g$ or $\frac{28}{g}$
16. $25 - n$

Page 119

1–4. Answers will vary. One possible answer is given.

1. The subtraction is the difference of 16 and 7. The division is the quotient of the difference and 3. Word expression: the quotient of the difference of 16 and 7 divided by 3.
2. The multiplication is the product of 5 and 9. The addition is the sum of 20 and the product. Word expression: the sum of 20 and the product of 5 and 9.
3. The expression is the difference of two terms. The first term is the product of 2 and e, and the second term is f. Word expression: the difference of 2 times e and f.
4. The expression is a sum of three terms. The first term is 8, the second term is the product of 6 and q, and the third term is q. Word expression: the sum of 8, the product of 6 and q, and q.
5. Terms: $11r$ and $7s$; coefficient in $11r$, 11; coefficient in $7s$, 7
6. Terms: $6g$ and h; coefficient in $6g$, 6; coefficient in h, 1
7. $6p$ and $5n$
8. The product of 4 and the sum of 15 and 20.

Page 120

1. 7.7
2. 17
3. $1\frac{3}{7}$
4. 9
5. 37
6. 15
7. $t - 19$
8. $34 + (13 + n)$

9–12. Answers will vary.

9. a number, t, decreased by 7
10. the sum of 29 and a number, n
11. 23 decreased by a number, r
12. a number, c, increased by the sum of 5 and 22
13. $n - 5.19$
14. 195
15. $A: d + 5; B: d - 2$

165

Page 121

1. 2.4
2. 11.5
3. 2.002
4. $\frac{49}{72}$
5. 2
6. 100
7. 12
8. $14x$
9. $\frac{n}{9}$
10. a number, z, divided by 11
11. the sum of a number, z, and 11
12. $4\frac{1}{2}$ lb
13. 15 years old
14. 1,320 ft or $\frac{1}{4}$ mile

Page 122

1. $c + 12$
2. $m + 5$
3. $s - 16$
4. $a - 33$

5–6. Expressions will vary. One possible answer is given.

5. a number, t, decreased by 7
6. a number, n, increased by 1.2
7. 14.5
8. 2
9. 14
10. 7
11. 25
12. 34.5
13. 5.5
14. 6
15. $p + 20$
16. $r - 3.25$
17. 40

Page 123

1. 3.21
2. 10.66
3. 91.681
4. 38.16
5. 1.91
6. 105.21
7. 97.3
8. 43.73
9. 98.652
10. 121.741
11. 54
12. 11.5
13. 93
14. 31.12
15. 0

16. 84
17. 21
18. 18
19. 12.6
20. 54.6
21. 38.98
22. 6.7
23. 11.06
24. 103.73
25. 134 lb
26. 9.935
27. 0
28. 3 times

Page 124

1. 115.2
2. 82.8
3. 450
4. 45.72
5. 8
6. 26
7. 212.5
8. 14.8
9. 120
10. 48
11. 216
12. 56
13. 5.16
14. 6.3
15. 15.87
16. 2.25
17. 7.938
18. 6.9
19. 2,338.3
20. 3.55
21. $\frac{d}{5}$; $2.25
22. $7s$; 35 mi
23. Check problem.

Page 125

1. 4
2. 38
3. $2\frac{3}{8}$
4. −16
5. −20
6. −2
7. −5
8. −14
9. 13.6
10. −11
11. −9
12. −10
13. 3
14. $\frac{1}{16}$

15. $\frac{13}{16}$
16. 16
17. $\frac{1}{8}$
18. 18
19. $\frac{13}{18}$
20. 25
21. $4\frac{1}{4}$
22. $6\frac{1}{4}$
23. $\frac{1}{32}$
24. $2\frac{1}{2}$
25. 90
26. $22\frac{1}{2}$
27. 60
28. 27.9
29. 12.6
30. 89.1
31. 51.84
32. 6.39
33. 234
34. 41.4
35. 0.18
36. 1
37. $b = 6 + 6$
38. $m + 2$; 5 mi
39. No. Possible explanation: subtraction is not commutative.

Page 126

1. 43
2. 70
3. 27
4. 27
5. 42
6. 90
7. 90
8. 34
9. 42
10. 42
11. 60
12. 12
13. 6
14. 6
15. 12
16. 6
17. 35
18. 20
19. 750
20. 750
21. 70
22. 5
23. 50
24. 120

25. 10
26. 10
27. 1
28. 25

Page 127

1. 9, 10, 11, 12; $x + 3$
2. 8, 10, 12; $2x$
3. 4, 5, 6, 7; $x - 4$
4. 5, 6, 7; $\frac{1}{3}x$
5. 1, $\frac{5}{4}$, $\frac{3}{2}$, $\frac{7}{4}$, 2; $\frac{1}{4}x$
6. 20, 24, 28, 32; $4x$
7. $y + 4$
8. $3y$
9. Relations will vary.

Page 128

1. $6y$
2. $11n$
3. $18m$
4. $25yz$
5. $6x$
6. $3a$
7. $7st$
8. $4m$
9. $80y$
10. $28b$
11. $44s$
12. $30mn$
13. x
14. $-10t$
15. $-10cd$
16. $-12v$
17. $5ab$
18. $-2t$
19. $4rs$
10. $-31y$
21. a
22. $\frac{2}{3}n$
23. $3\frac{1}{2}x$
24. $1\frac{1}{2}d$
25. $1.8b$
26. $4y$
27. k
28. $0.12t$
29. $9a$
30. $14xy$
31. $18m$
32. $10h$

Page 129

1. $2y$
2. a

3. $7rt$
4. $6w$
5. $-2h$
6. $-3yz$
7. $-7f$
8. $-9mn$
9. $-9x$
10. $-12g$
11. $-14z$
12. $-59b$
13. $5n$
14. $3p$
15. $-4k$
16. $-10r$
17. $2t$
18. $-6m$
19. $-11a$
20. $-27xy$
21. $4ab$
22. $4k$
23. $-t$
24. $-5x$
25. $\frac{1}{2}t$
26. $\frac{1}{5}x$
27. $\frac{1}{3}h$
28. b
29. $0.18n$
30. $0.5a$
31. $0.7k$
32. $1.8st$

Page 130

1. $-5xy$
2. $7mn$
3. $-9k$
4. $0.4c$
5. $-10pq$
6. $-2h$
7. $-v$
8. $22ab$
9. $-0.7n$
10. b
11. $14pr$
12. $-18wx$
13. $14z$
14. $4lm$
15. $-5u$
16. $-10s$
17. $5z$
18. $-6.9u$
19. $-9rp$
20. $22b$
21. $-30ty$

22. $-15c$
23. $-0.1c$
24. $-22fg$
25. $24r$
26. $-88h$
27. $-25ds$
28. $-18j$
29. $-en$
30. $1.49i$
31. $-11w$
32. $-29x$
33. $16kl$
34. $-23dh$
35. $-2.3s$
36. 0

Page 131

1. $7a$
2. $4g$
3. $-x$
4. $3y$
5. $2m$
6. 0
7. $3a + 3b$
8. $4s + 12t$
9. $6ab - 11ac$
10. $8m - 2r$
11. $-13k + 11$
12. $5x + 2$
13. $23xy - 18$
14. $-8f + 10$
15. $rs + st$
16. $-7g + 3$
17. $e + 6ef$
18. $-13x$
19. $12bc + 21$
20. $-105p$
21. $75r - 89$

Page 132

1. $4h$
2. $7x + 7$
3. $16 + 4p$
4. $y^2 + 5y$
5. $13h + 15$
6. $19 + 4n$
7. $18 + 10k$
8. $15m + 10$
9. $6g + 6h$
10–12. Answers will vary. One possible answer is given.
10. $4(d + 2)$
11. $7(3p + 5q)$
12. $9(2x + y)$

Answer Key
Core Skills Math, Grade 6

13. $27n + 100$; $316
14. $n + 4n$; $5n$

Page 133

1. equivalent
2. equivalent
3. not equivalent
4. not equivalent
5. equivalent
6. not equivalent
7. equivalent
8. equivalent
9. equivalent
10. not equivalent
11. not equivalent
12. equivalent
13. $3b + 3s$
14. equivalent

Page 134

1. $n = 5$
2. $b = 45$
3. $x = 6\frac{1}{3}$
4. $y = \frac{27}{56}$
5. $y = 55$
6. $c = 1.3$
7. $n + 19 = 221$; $n = 202$
8. $n + 1\frac{2}{3} = 8$; $n = 6\frac{1}{3}$
9. $n + 6\frac{1}{5} = 8\frac{2}{3}$; $2\frac{7}{15}$
10. $n + 5.4 = 23.1$; $n = 17.7$
11. $n + (3 + 2.6) = 9$; 3.4
12. $n + 29 = 113$; $n = 84$
13. $n + 2\frac{2}{3} = 4\frac{1}{2}$; $n = 1\frac{5}{6}$; $1\frac{5}{6}$ miles
14. fewer than
15. 3
16. 0.4
17. 70

Page 135

1. $a = 72$
2. $x = 74$
3. $x = 10\frac{3}{8}$
4. $c = 109$
5. $y = 14$
6. $b = 6\frac{11}{12}$
7. $a = 3\frac{13}{18}$
8. $c = 8.505$
9. $b = 28$
10. $m - 5 = 22$; $m = 27$; 27 students
11. $m + 22.05 = 58.95$; $m = 36.90$; $36.90
12. $p - \frac{1}{6} = \frac{4}{6}$; $\frac{5}{6}$

Page 136

1. subtract 2
2. add 9
3. subtract 24
4. subtract 10
5. subtract 13
6. add 26
7. subtract 1.7
8. subtract 7.6
9. add 3.34
10. add 8.5
11. subtract 43.8
12. subtract 23.4
13. $x = 9$
14. $n = 6$
15. $t = 21$
16. $t = 13$
17. $m = 26$
18. $r = 3.5$
19. 11,656
20. 12,359
21. 41,359
22. 108,133
23. 20,478
24. $12 + t$
25. $r - 9$
26. $x + 4.6$
27. $9.7 - u$
28–31. Answers may vary. One possible answer is given.
28. 13.98 fewer than a number, w
29. the sum of a number, c, and 235
30. 12.8 more than a number, d
31. s less than 7.3

Page 137

1. $n = 7$
2. $y = 64$
3. $x = 9$
4. $y = 7$
5. $n = 16$
6. $x = 34$
7. $n = 7$
8. $y = 2$
9. $b = 16$
10. $n = 56$
11. $n = 12$
12. $r = 13$
13. $k = 4$
14. $a = 2$
15. $b = 7.5$
16. $n - 19 = 84$; $n = 103$; 103 cards
17. $3n = 12$; $n = 4$; 4 miles per hour

18. $r = \frac{1}{2}$
19. $z = 0$
20. $n = 1$

Page 138

1. $x = 36$
2. $a = 35$
3. $n = 87$
4. $n = 30$
5. $x = 120$
6. $b = 135$
7. $n = 119$
8. $x = 24$
9. $y = 165$
10. $e = 180$
11. $a = 100$
12. $b = 112$
13. $\frac{n}{8} = 2.5$; $n = 20$
14. $n + 6.05 = 12.4$; $n = 6.35$
15. $n = \frac{1}{4} \times 36 = 9$; 9 years old
16. $\frac{1}{3} n = 24$; $n = 72$; 72 hours
17. about 20
18. about 40
19. about 3

Page 139

1. division
2. division
3. multiplication
4. multiplication
5. multiply both sides by 4
6. divide by 2
7. multiply by 3
8. divide by 10
9. multiply by 5
10. divide by 8
11. divide by 5
12. divide by 15
13. multiply by 8
14. multiply by 14
15. divide by 35
16. multiply by 3
17. multiply by 13
18. divide by 12
19. divide by 63
20. multiply by 116
21. $t = 12$
22. $n = 13$
23. $d = 40$
24. $x = 14$
25. $w = 105$
26. $h = 51$

Page 140

1. addition
2. subtraction
3. subtraction
4. addition
5. addition
6. subtraction
7. $x = 98$
8. $y = 934$
9. $m = 58$
10. $x = \frac{3}{5}$
11. $t = 1\frac{3}{4}$
12. $q = 4\frac{3}{4}$
13. $x = \frac{5}{14}$
14. $c = \frac{5}{6}$
15. $n = 15\frac{1}{4}$
16. $z = 2\frac{1}{8}$
17. $d = 1\frac{1}{6}$
18. $m = \frac{4}{11}$
19. $r = 57,546$
20. $s = 136,889$
21. $246 + d$
22. 129 peaches
23. 6
24. 2
25. 12
26. 7
27. 2^4
28. 5×7
29. 2×5^2
30. $3^2 \times 7$
31. no
32. yes
33. yes
34. no

Page 141

Answers to Exercises **4**, **5**, **7**, and **10** may vary.

1. add 11 and -8
2. add -9 and 4
3. add 6 to each side
4. subtract 3 from each side
5. add 16 to each side
6. add 7 to each side
7. subtract 4 from each side
8. subtract 35 from each side
9. add 8 to each side
10. add 4 to each side
11. 8
12. 23

13. -2
14. -1
15. -2
16. 40
17. 17
18. -4
19. -10
20. -2
21. -15
22. -7
23. 7
24. 10
25. -10
26. 22
27. 11
28. -3
29. 21
30. $585
31. -5°C
32. -5, -3
33. 7, 11

Page 142

1. 8; 1; ≠; not a solution
2. solution
3. not a solution
4. not a solution
5. solution
6. solution
7. not a solution
8. solution
9. not a solution
10. $p = 7$ is a solution; $p = 13$ is not a solution. Terrance needs to score 7 point to win.
11. $s = 32$ is not a solution; $s = 80$ is a solution; There are 80 sheets in a full roll.

Page 143

1. $c; p; c; p - 3$
2. $c; p; c; p + 6$
3. $b; n; b; 12n$
4. $t; b; t; b - 2$
5. $s; a; s; 10a$
6. $e = 45n$
7. $s = 100 + c$

Page 144

1. 12, 30, 48
2. 3, 8, 13
3. 13, 16, 19
4. $y = 8x$; 24
5. $y = \frac{x}{2}$; 11

6. $y = x + 5$; 19
7. $y = x - 9$; 8
8. $y = 11x + 4$
9. $y = 24x$; 120 shrimp

Page 145

1. 5, 6, 7
2. 9, 12, 15
3. 6, 4, 2
4. 5, 7, 9
5–6. Check graphs.
7. $5s + 1$
8. 51 magazines
9. Answers will vary.

Page 146

1. 3, 4, 5

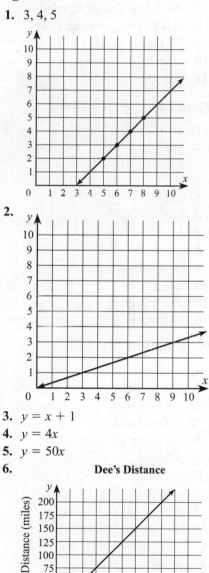

3. $y = x + 1$
4. $y = 4x$
5. $y = 50x$
6. **Dee's Distance**

Page 147

1. $w > 4$, where w is the width in centimeters and is a positive number
2. $s \geq 10$, where s is any whole number
3. $m < 5$, where m is any positive number
4. $h > 2.5$, where h is any positive number
5. $t \leq -3$, where t is any negative number
6–9. Answers will vary. One possible answer is given.
6. k is less than -7
7. z is greater than or equal to 14
8. m is less than or equal to $2\frac{3}{5}$
9. f is greater than 0.24
10. $m \geq 30$
11. $c \leq 25$

Page 148

1. no
2. yes
3. no
4. no
5. yes
6. no
7. b
8. c
9–12. Check number lines.
13. $x > 15$
14. $y + 25 = 100$
15. -2 and -1

Page 149

1. solution
2. not a solution
3. not a solution
4. not a solution
5. not a solution
6. solution
7. solution
8. solution
9. not a solution
10–14. Answers will vary. One possible answer is given.
10. $k = 0$; $k = 1$
11. $z = -1$; $z = 1$
12. $f = -5$; $f = -5.5$
13. 92; 95
14. $20; $19